JOURNEYING WITH MARK:
REFLECTIONS ON THE SUNDAY GOSPEL READINGS FOR YEAR B

Journeying
with Mark

Reflections on the Sunday Gospel
Readings for Year B

MARTIN HOGAN

VERITAS

Published 2017 by
Veritas Publications
7–8 Lower Abbey Street
Dublin 1
Ireland
publications@veritas.ie
www.veritas.ie

ISBN 978 1 84730 811 5

10 9 8 7 6 5 4 3 2 1

Designed and typeset by Padraig McCormack, Veritas
Printed in the Republic of Ireland by SPRINT-print Ltd, Dublin

Veritas books are printed on paper made from the wood pulp of managed forests. For every tree felled, at least one tree is planted, thereby renewing natural resources.

Contents

Sacred Triduum

Easter

Ordinary Time

Introduction

During Year B, the Sunday Gospel readings are mostly taken from the Gospel of Mark. A great deal of Mark's Gospel will be read over these Sundays, sometimes entire chapters, and, at the very least, sections of each of the sixteen chapters. What kind of Gospel did Mark the Evangelist write? The Gospel of Mark is the earliest and the shortest of the four Gospels. Much of the best known and most loved material about Jesus is missing from this Gospel, such as the story of Jesus' birth, the parables of the prodigal son and the good samaritan, the teaching of the Sermon on the Mount, the Resurrection appearances of Jesus. Yet, scholars who study the Gospels as literature often point to Mark as the masterpiece of the Gospels. When it is read in public from beginning to end by a competent performer it can make a powerful impact.

One way of exploring the overall shape of Mark's story of Jesus is by attending to the various locations that are referred to in the Gospel. Mark's Gospel begins 'in the wilderness' where John was baptising, and where Jesus, having been baptised by John, was tempted (1:1–13). These opening thirteen verses can be understood as a kind of prologue to the Gospel. If location is taken as a guide, three main sections of Mark's Gospel can be identified in the remainder of the Gospel. In 1:14 Jesus enters Galilee where he remains for the following seven chapters. This gives us the Galilean section of the Gospel (1:14–8:26). In this section, Jesus is portrayed as working many miracles. He appears as the promised 'Mighty One' through whom God is powerfully at work, releasing people from all that oppresses and dehumanises them. Within this Galilean section, from 4:35 to 8:26, Jesus travels at times beyond Galilee towards pagan territory, indicating that his mission, while primarily to Israel, has ultimately the Gentiles in view as well.

After the Galilean section there follows the 'way section' in 8:27–10:52. The first mention of the phrase 'on the way' occurs in 8:27 and is repeated over the following two chapters, occurring for the last time in 10:52. During this section of the Gospel, Jesus is on his way to Jerusalem. A turning point in Mark's Gospel is to be found at the beginning of this section (8:27–30). Jesus asks his disciples the decisive question 'Who do you say that I am?' and Peter answers, 'You are the Christ'. Jesus then immediately begins to speak of himself as the Son of Man who must undergo great suffering and be killed, indicating what kind of 'Christ' he will be. Jesus' reference to himself as the suffering Son of Man sets the tone for the section to follow. In this section of the Gospel Jesus is 'on the way' to the city of Jerusalem where he will undergo his passion and death. On the way, Jesus is primarily in the company of his disciples and his teaching is addressed to them. He struggles to open the eyes of his disciples to his identity as the Son of Man who must be rejected by the religious leaders and be killed. He also struggles to get them to accept the implications of this for themselves as his followers. They too must travel the way of the cross. Yet, they refuse to see what Jesus is trying to show them. The story of the healing of the blind man at the beginning and end of this section symbolises Jesus' efforts to heal the blindness of his disciples.

In 11:1 Jesus reaches Jerusalem, and this begins the Jerusalem section of the Gospel (11:1–15:47). The following chapters are an account of his brief ministry in Jerusalem (11:1–13:37), culminating in the narrative of his passion and death (14:1–15:47). Whereas in Galilee, Jesus performed many miracles, in Jerusalem he performs none. As he enters his passion, he becomes more and more passive; he suffers as the victim of the actions of others. Yet, he is not totally passive. He willingly goes to his death in fulfilment of his mission. Corresponding to the prologue at the beginning of the Gospel, the last eight verses can be considered an epilogue (16:1–8). The Gospel that begins in the wilderness concludes at a tomb, another kind of wilderness. The women come to the tomb to anoint the body of Jesus and discover that his body is not there. In the Judean wilderness, which is a place of death, John the Baptist made a promise of new life (1:7-8). At the tomb, another place of death, a young man makes an announcement of new life (16:6-7). The emergence of new life in the wilderness is an underlying theme of Mark's Gospel. The young man also announces that Jesus is going back to Galilee ahead of his disciples where they will see him. The women fled from the tomb and said nothing to anyone of what they had seen and heard because they were overcome with terror and amazement (16:8). This is the strange ending of Mark's Gospel which has perplexed commentators; it is an open ending. Perhaps the Evangelist is calling on the reader or hearer of the Gospel to pick up where the women left off; we are to go and proclaim the good news of Easter. The word of promise and hope in the previous verse (16:7) is Mark's final message. The risen Jesus will be faithful to his failing disciples.

Mark's Gospel offers the most human portrait of Jesus, of all four Gospels. Like any human being, Jesus becomes tired (6:31) and hungry (11:12). He feels a wide range of human emotions including anger (3:5), amazement (6:6), compassion (6:34), discouragement (8:12), indignation (10:14), love (10:21) and grief (14:34). Jesus does not know everything (13:32) and his power is sometimes limited by others' lack of faith (6:5). Matthew and Luke, and especially John, give us a more exalted picture of Jesus. Yet, Mark is aware that Jesus, while being fully human, has a unique relationship with God. He alone is 'Son of God'. Mark opens his Gospel by stating that Jesus is the 'Christ, the Son of God' (1:1). It is in and through his humanity, especially his broken humanity, that he reveals himself to be 'Son of God'.

The opening words of Jesus in Mark are the key to understanding Jesus' identity, 'The time is fulfilled and the kingdom of God has come near' (1:14-15). The promise of the prophets in the Jewish scriptures is now being fulfilled. God's kingdom is at hand. The term 'kingdom of God' is not primarily a spatial reality but a dynamic one. Jesus declares that the powerful presence of God's rule has arrived in his person and ministry. The visible impact of God's rule in Jesus shows itself in his deeds, such as, his healing the sick (1:21–2:12), his feeding the hungry (6:30–44; 8:1–10), his table fellowship with sinners (2:13–17), his gathering of a new kind of community (3:31–5). During his Galilean ministry, Jesus speaks and acts with the power and authority of God. He is the 'powerful one' who enters the strong man's house (that of Satan), ties up the strong man and plunders his property (4:27). The fullness of God's rule will come when Jesus returns as the glorious Son of Man. Meanwhile, Jesus' proclamation of God's kingdom demands an appropriate response: repenting and believing in the Good News Jesus brings. 'To repent' is to break with the past, so as to turn towards God. 'To believe' is to recognise God ruling in Jesus and to entrust oneself to God powerfully present in Jesus. However, God's action comes first; God takes the initiative. God is reigning in a life-giving way through Jesus. This calls for a human response. God's action makes human action possible. Those who respond now to the presence of God's reign in Jesus will inherit that kingdom in all its fullness when Jesus returns.

Mark emphasises that the one through whom God was powerfully working in Galilee is also the one who was crucified in weakness in Jerusalem. The 'powerful one' is also the one who dies in shame and weakness. The cross is central to Mark's depiction of Jesus, especially from 8:27 onwards. The whole of Mark's Gospel progresses inexorably towards Jesus' passion and death. The plot to kill Jesus is introduced much earlier in the narrative than in the other Gospels (3:6). From about half way through the Gospel (8:31) Jesus begins to speak of himself as the Son of Man who must undergo great suffering and be put to death. More than a third of the Gospel is taken up with the events of Jesus' last week (11:1–16:8). For Mark, God who was powerfully at work through the Galilean ministry of Jesus is even more powerfully at work through the death of Jesus. Paradoxically, the weakness of Jesus is the greatest demonstration of God's rule at work in the world. The cross of Jesus reveals the shape of the reign of God. It shows that the reign of God does not come without persecution, without daily dying, without self-emptying service. For Mark, it is above all on the cross that Jesus reveals his identity most fully. It is then that the suffering Son of Man is revealed as the faithful Son of God. It is not possible for people to really grasp what it means to say that Jesus is the Christ, the Son of God until he is crucified. Ironically, the Roman centurion is the only one to recognise the truth of Jesus' identity as he hangs from the cross (15:39).

The cross is also the defining symbol of what it means to be a disciple of Jesus in Mark's Gospel. The disciple is someone who walks in the way of Jesus, the way of self-emptying service of others, even though that will inevitably involve the way of the cross. In his portrait of Jesus' disciples Mark highlights their failure to understand Jesus. In the Galilean section of the Gospel they struggle to grasp who Jesus is (4:35–41). In the 'way section' of the Gospel they fail to grasp Jesus' references to himself as the suffering Son of Man and its implications for themselves as disciples. If the Galilean and, especially, the way section of the Gospel reveal their lack of understanding, the Jerusalem section reveals their lack of loyalty. Judas betrays Jesus, Peter denies him and the remaining disciples all desert him. Mark's portrait of the disciples may have served a pastoral purpose. He was probably writing to a community that had recently come through an experience of suffering and trial. Many in the community may have been coming to terms with their own failure to confess Jesus publicly when their faith was put to the test. Mark's portrait of Jesus' disciples would have been a reassuring word for his church. Even the first disciples, in whom Jesus had invested so much time and energy, failed. Yet, Jesus was faithful to them; after rising from the dead, he went on to meet them again in Galilee. Mark wanted to assure his community that they too would experience the Lord's faithfulness, in spite of past failures. The divine forgiveness and love that is extended to all through Jesus' death and Resurrection is not diminished because of human failure.

One of the striking features of Mark's Gospel is that in contrast to the disciples, the 'insiders', it is the more marginal characters in Mark's story, the 'outsiders' who show what it means to be a true disciple, such as the pagan woman (7:24–30), the blind beggar (10:46–52), the poor widow (12:41–4), the woman who anoints Jesus (14:1–11) and the Roman centurion (15:39).

Many people like to anchor their daily time of quiet prayer in a scripture passage. One way of doing this is to prayerfully reflect on the Gospel reading for the following Sunday. For many years I have found it helpful to take the Gospel reading of the Sunday as a basis for prayer. It is my hope that these reflections might be a help to those who wish to spend a time of prayer with the Gospel reading of the following Sunday. Many of our parishes now have *Lectio Divina* prayer groups, whose members take the Sunday Gospel as the focus of their time of prayer together. These reflections may be a resource for such groups. Priests who have to prepare a Sunday homily week in and week out may also find these reflections helpful. The Lord speaks in a unique way to each person who prayerfully sits before his word in the Gospels. These reflections are my effort to share with others how I have heard the Lord's word through the Gospel readings of the Sundays for Liturgical Year B. I hope that some of these reflections might serve as a small prompt for others to hear how the Lord may be speaking to them through these same Gospel readings.

ADVENT

First Sunday of Advent   *A watchful waiting for the Lord*

Is 63:16-17; 64:1, 3-8; 1 Cor 1:3-9; Mk 13:33-7

The first Sunday of Advent has come around again. The Jesse tree and the Advent wreath are in place. The green of Ordinary Time has given way to the more sombre violet of Advent. The liturgical mood has changed a little. We drop the Gloria from our Sunday Mass for this season. Liturgically, the Church holds itself in reserve somewhat, until the great outbreak of joy at the feast of Christmas. Advent is a quiet, reflective, prayerful season. We are in a waiting, expectant mode. It is the season when we wait for the Lord, when we pray *Maranatha*, 'Come, Lord Jesus'.

We wait for the Lord's coming because we know that we need the Lord's coming. People who are waiting usually have a sense of something or someone missing. That is the case whether it is a parent waiting for their son or daughter to come through the arrival gate at the airport, or a couple waiting for their child to be born, or a sick person in hospital waiting for an expected visitor. The experience of waiting brings home to us that we are incomplete. It reminds us that at some deep level of our lives we are in need, we need others.

The season of Advent reminds us of our need of the Lord. It is the season when we stand with open hearts and invite the Lord to come and to bring us to completion. We begin Advent acknowledging our need of that completion, our need of the Lord's coming. The first reading of the first Sunday of Advent this year gives us words to express that need, 'We have all withered like leaves and our sins blew us away like the wind.' We have all become familiar with the withered leaves of autumn these recent months. The words of the prophet Isaiah today suggest that these withered leaves are symbols of all that is withered in our lives. In recent years, we have become more aware of the withered areas of our Church's life. As a Church, we have felt more keenly our need of the Lord's coming. Out of that sense of need we pray with greater vigour than usual, 'Come, Lord Jesus', or we might pray the prayer of today's responsorial psalm, 'Visit this vine and protect it, the vine your right hand has chosen.' The vine is an image of the people of God, an image of the Church. We pray for a fresh visitation of the Lord to his church, and a greater openness on all our parts to receive the Lord's visitation.

That first reading of Advent today is a lament, a communal cry to the Lord, out of a shared sense of having failed the Lord. Yet, at the end of the reading there is the conviction that the Lord is the potter who can make something new out of his flawed people. He can take material that looks unpromising and with it create a work of art. That is also our conviction as we begin Advent. We invite the Lord to come and shape us anew. To acknowledge how out of shape we are is itself to create an opening for the Lord to come. Recognising what is wrong, acknowledging our need, therefore, does not leave us discouraged. We are full of hope in the Lord who does not give up on his people but continues to shape and mould them. Advent is a hopeful season, a time when we wait in joyful hope for the coming of our Saviour Jesus Christ.

This hopeful waiting is not in any sense a sitting back and doing nothing approach, as if the Lord is going to do it all for us. People who are waiting for someone dear to them are anything but laid back. If you watch people at airports waiting for loved ones to arrive, their faces are full of alertness. That is the kind of waiting that is associated with Advent, and that Jesus calls for in the Gospel reading today. 'Be on your guard, stay awake,' he says. As we wait, we are alert and attentive. We are attentive to the task the Lord has given us. We each have been given the task of growing in our relationship with the Lord, being in prayerful communion with him, witnessing to him in our daily lives. The Lord asks us to keep to that task as we wait for him, to stay at our post as it were, not to get discouraged or to lose heart. We have the assurance of St Paul in the second reading that as we keep to our task, the Lord provides us with the help we need to do that task well. Paul tells us: 'You will not be without any of the gifts of the Spirit while you are waiting for our Lord Jesus Christ.' The Lord graces us for the task he gives to us, while inviting us to wait in joyful hope for his coming which is assured. That is the spirit of Advent. We pray that in the coming four weeks, we would show ourselves to be Advent people, alive with the spirit of Advent.

Second Sunday of Advent
New life in the wilderness

Is 40:1–5, 9–11; 2 Pt 3:8–14; Mk 1:1–8

One of the images that we find in the readings for the second Sunday of Advent is that of the wilderness. When I was on a pilgrimage to the Holy Land some years ago, I was struck by the Judean wilderness. The land between Jerusalem and the River Jordan and especially down towards the Dead Sea is a true wilderness. It is barren and rocky and hilly. There are very few signs of life there. Occasionally you could see a Bedouin camp with a small flock of goats alongside. It was down towards the River Jordan not far from the Dead Sea that John the Baptist would have engaged in his ministry. He was the voice crying in that wilderness.

People would rarely have gone to the wilderness in large numbers. It was a place to be avoided or, at the very most, it was a place to be got through quickly on the way from one centre of population, like Jerusalem, to another, like Jericho. Yet, the Gospel reading today tells us that 'all Judea and all the people of Jerusalem made their way' to John the Baptist in the wilderness. Why did such large numbers leave the relative comfort of their homes to head out into an inhospitable place to listen to this austere man of the wilderness? They were somehow drawn by John's preaching of a Baptism of repentance for the forgiveness of sins. John was proclaiming the gift of God's merciful love to all who acknowledged their need of it. That message somehow struck a chord with people. It was a spiritual thirst and hunger which led them out into the wilderness to meet with John the Baptist. They were seeking and finding God in the wilderness. They were experiencing the wilderness as an opportunity to make a new beginning, to set out on a new journey, what the Gospel reading and the first reading call 'the way of the Lord'.

The presence of God in the wilderness is central to today's second reading as well. The prophet Isaiah spoke those very consoling words to the people of Israel in exile. The time of exile was a real wilderness experience. Even though they were living in a city, they experienced a wilderness of spirit because they had been forcibly removed from their geographical and spiritual home. The prophet announces that God is with them in their wilderness experience and that he will come to lead them through the physical wilderness back to their homeland. The prophet announces, 'Here is your God,' coming with power, not as the world understands power, but with the power of love, like a shepherd gathering lambs in his arms and holding them against his breast. Like John the Baptist, the prophet Isaiah announces new life in the wilderness, only in this case the wilderness in question is a wilderness of heart, a wilderness of the spirit. Whereas in the Gospel reading the people journeyed into the physical wilderness to experience God, in the first reading the prophet Isaiah announces that God is journeying with power into their own personal and communal wilderness. Because of that, the wilderness will prove to be a moment of new beginning for all the people. New life will emerge in the wilderness.

We have all had our own wilderness experiences. We might think of times when we were deprived of the normal resources that always gave us life. An experience of bereavement is such a time. We are deprived of the presence that has sustained us. The landscape of our lives suddenly seems harsh and barren. There are other experiences of loss which have a similar effect on us, whether it is the loss of a treasured friendship or the loss of a job, or the loss of our good name. An experience of failure can be a wilderness time. We begin to feel fragile and vulnerable as people do who spend time in the physical wilderness. Many people struggle with depression, whether in a mild or more serious form. They enter a wilderness of mind and spirit which can drain them of life and energy. The prospect of Christmas can be depressing for many people, especially for those who have suffered a recent bereavement. As well as our own personal wilderness, we can be caught up in a form of communal wilderness, like the people in exile. As a Church, we have been through and are still in a wilderness time.

The message of the readings for this second Sunday of Advent is that, regardless of the kind of wilderness in which we find ourselves, there is the promise of new life in the wilderness, because God is always present in the wilderness. When we are at our weakest the strong arm of the Lord is there to gather us and to empower us to set out on a new journey. In times of crisis, we long for newness, what the second reading refers to as 'the new heavens and new earth'. The Lord will respond to that longing in our hearts if, like the people of Jerusalem in the Gospel reading, we go in search of him.

Third Sunday of Advent

The question of identity

Is 61:1–2, 10–11; 1 Th 5:16–24; Jn 1:6–8, 19–28

Some of the questions that people ask us in the course of our lives can be answered quickly, without having to give too much thought to the answer. A visitor to our capital city might ask us where the Botanic Gardens are, and we immediately give them directions. There are other questions that we really need a lot of time to think about. Someone might ask us if we could intervene in a family dispute. We need time to think out our answer to that request, time perhaps to talk it over with one or two others. Then there are still other questions which are so deep that we might never really get around to answering them fully at all. These are questions that we live with, as it were. They don't go away. From time to time we get some light on them, but we often find ourselves going back to them. We grapple with them over time.

The question that the Pharisees put to John the Baptist in the Gospel reading this evening, 'Who are you?', might come into that category. The question of our identity 'Who am I?' is one we return to more than once in our lives. John the Baptist seems to have had great clarity about who he was. As a result, he did not claim to be someone he wasn't. He said to his questioners, 'I am not the Christ.' He knew he wasn't even Elijah or the Prophet who was to come at the end of time. Part of knowing who we are involves knowing who we are not. People can sometimes be put under pressure to become someone they are not. They can yield to that pressure to please those they love and respect. After many years, they can discover that they have been trying to become the person others expected them to be, rather than being themselves. They can come to realise that they have been putting a lot of energy into living up to the expectations of others. In the process, they may feel they have lost touch somewhat with who they really are. It is likely that some of the followers of John the Baptist expected him to be the Messiah, and looked to him to become the Messiah. John resisted that pressure because he knew who he was. He had come to understand that he was a voice who prepared people to meet the Messiah. He was not the word; he was the voice who helped people to recognise the presence of the word made flesh in their midst.

Rather than becoming the person others wanted him to be, John the Baptist was content to be the person God wanted him to be. He knew that God gave him his identity, not any human being. It was God who called him to be the voice who prepares the way for God's son. The question, 'Who are you?', is really the question, 'Who does God want you to be?' In the second reading, Paul refers to 'what God expects you to do'. Even more fundamental than what God expects you to do is who God expects you to be. God gives us our identity. God calls us by our name. We try to hear the Lord call our name, and it is in responding to that call that we become our true selves, we find ourselves. The answer to the question 'Who are you?' or 'Who does God want you to be?' will be unique to each of us. No two of us will answer that question in the same way, because God gives each of us a unique identity.

Yet, the unique identity God gives to each of us has a common element. God calls each of us to become Christ-like; he calls us to grow up into his son. John the Baptist knew that his calling was to make Christ known. That is also our calling too. We are to make Christ known by allowing him to live in us. We live out that calling in a way that is unique to each of us. To the extent that our own unique lives witness to Christ, we become the person that God wants us to become, we become our true selves. Such a Christ-like person, in the words of the first reading, will bring good news to the poor, healing to the broken and freedom to the captives. These are some of the signs of the Christ-like person. We pray this Advent for the grace to be true to this God-given identity.

Fourth Sunday of Advent   *God's disturbing presence*

2 Sm 7:1-5, 8-12, 14, 16; Rm 16:25-7; Lk 1:26-38

Christmas day is almost upon us. Most of us are busy getting ready for Christmas. There are last minute presents to be bough, food to be prepared. Preparations are afoot for visitors. We will probably all be travelling over the next few days, visiting family and friends and being visited by them. Some of us will be travelling to our Christmas dinner. There is a lot of coming and going these days.

In these busy days, the Gospel reading for this fourth Sunday of Advent presents us with a scene which is anything but busy. It is a quiet, mysterious and, yet, hugely momentous scene. The evangelist Luke attempts to capture in narrative form the moment in Mary's life when she consented to what God was asking of her, when she said 'yes' to God's call. Those very personal moments in our lives when we have a strong sense of God's presence to us, of God touching our lives in a very powerful way, are difficult to talk about or to write about. However, as Luke describes the momentous exchange between God and Mary in that small house in Nazareth of Galilee, Mary's initial response to God's approach was one of great unease. 'She was deeply disturbed by these words', even though the words, in themselves, were very reassuring, 'Rejoice, so highly favoured! The Lord is with you.' Yet, Mary's reaction is a perfectly understandable one. God's ways are not our ways. God's thoughts are not our thoughts. Any deep experience of God will always be disturbing in some way. Any kind of meeting with God, with the Lord, can never be a completely comfortable experience. Yes, God is love, but authentic love will always stretch us in some way, and call us beyond where we are. It is because an experience of God will always be disturbing to some degree that we can find it difficult to pray. Yet, when God disturbs us, the root of that disturbance is love and the fruit of it is new life.

Luke captures a second movement in Mary's heart in response to this approach of God. When God begins to make clear to her what he is asking of her, she begins to question. The angel said to her, 'You are to conceive and bear a son ... He will be great and will be called Son of the Most High.' Mary's response to that news was, 'How can this come about, since I am a virgin?' According to Luke, this would not be the last time she would question what God was doing in her life. Luke tells us that at the time of the birth of Jesus, Mary treasured all the words of the shepherds and 'pondered them in her heart'. At the time when she and Joseph found Jesus in the temple, Luke states that 'they did not understand what he said to them', and that his mother 'treasured all these things in her heart'. From the first moment of God's call to her, Mary had to live with many questions, not all of which would be answered during her son's lifetime.

Luke's portrait of Mary suggests that deep faith can find expression in profound religious questioning. Sometimes when people find themselves beginning to question their faith they think that they are losing their faith. On the contrary, questioning our faith can lead to a deepening of our faith. Part of the journey of faith is learning to live with questions. What more disturbing question could there be than the question which, in the Gospels of Mark and Matthew, is to be found on the lips of Jesus as he dies, 'My God, my God, why have you forsaken me?' As people of faith, we will often find ourselves asking the question Mary asked in today's Gospel reading, 'How can this come about?' 'How can this be?' The onset of serious illness in our own lives or in the life of a close family member can leave us asking this question. In the Gospel reading Mary received an answer to her question. We will not always receive an answer to our questions; we may have to live with them for a long time. Jesus' question from the cross was answered by the Resurrection. Some of our questions will only be fully answered when we share in the Lord's risen life.

The third movement within Mary that Luke depicts is that of surrendering to what God wants of her, 'Let what you have said be done to me.' This is perhaps the most difficult movement of all, for all of us. In the second reading, Paul refers to 'the way the eternal God wants things to be'. Mary gave herself over to the way the eternal God wanted things to be. Mary did not choose to be mother of God's son, God chose her. This was not Mary's way, it was God's way, to which Mary said 'yes', with profound consequences for all of us. As Christians, we spend our lives trying to discern how God wants things to be and, then, struggling to live accordingly. It is Mary's son who reveals to us how God wants things to be. It is the Holy Spirit, who overshadowed Mary, who gives us the power to live in accordance with how God wants things to be.

CHRISTMAS

Christmas: Midnight Mass

A child given to us

Is 9:1-7; Ti 2:11-14; Lk 2:1-14

Earlier this week we had the shortest day of the year. I always find the shortest day of the year significant. The realisation that from this day onwards, light is making a comeback always gives me a lift of some kind. The passage tombs in Newgrange may have been designed around the conviction that just as darkness is at its most intense, light is also in evidence. There is a chant from the monastery of Taizé in France which goes, 'Within our darkest night, you kindle a flame that never dies away, that never dies away.'

It is fitting that the Christian feast of Christmas coincides with the time of year when light begins to increase after the increasing presence of darkness for the previous six months. The opening verses of our first reading express the tone and meaning of tonight's feast, 'The people who walked in darkness has seen a great light; on those who live in a land of deep shadow a light has shone.' It goes on to identify this great light with the birth of a child, 'For there is a child born for us, a son given to us … and this is the name they will give him: Wonder-Counsellor, Mighty God, Eternal Father, Prince of Peace.' It is almost as if those lines, written many centuries before the birth of Jesus, were composed with this event in mind. They capture so beautifully why we are gathered here this night.

There are only two times in the Church's liturgical year when we gather in church long after darkness has fallen. The first is the Easter Vigil when we celebrate the night or the early morning when Jesus rose from the dead. The second is Christmas night when we celebrate the birth of Jesus. The Gospel reading that we have just heard suggests that Jesus' birth took place at night, 'In the countryside close by there were shepherds who lived in the fields and took it in turns to watch their flocks during the night. The angel of the Lord appeared to them …

and said, "Listen, I bring you news of great joy". The shepherds were the first to hear the good news that in the darkness of the night a great light has shone. It is the birth of Jesus, the light of the world, that brings us together in the darkness of this winter night. In the words of that Taizé chant we celebrate the good news that, within our darkest night, God has kindled a flame that never dies away.

Over the past four weeks we have been gradually lighting our Advent wreath. Tonight, it is fully lit. All five candles are burning, as is fitting for this great feast of light. Our focus now shifts from the Advent wreath, to the crib. The birth of a child brings a special light into the lives of the child's parents and family. The birth of this child, the child of Mary and Joseph, brings a special light into the lives of every one of us. We are all caught up in the birth of this child. In the words of Isaiah again in that first reading, 'There is a child born for us, a son given to us', and in the words of the angel to the shepherds in the Gospel reading, 'Today in the town of David a saviour has been born to you.' This child was not born simply to Mary and Joseph; he was born to all of us, for all of us. This child is God's gift to each one of us, to all of humanity. In the words of Paul that open tonight's second reading, 'God's grace has been revealed, and it has made salvation possible for the whole human race.' We are all deeply invested in the birth of the child which we celebrate this night.

We could not all be present at the actual birth of Jesus, but we are all invited to celebrate this birth, because Jesus was born for each of us. What was announced to the shepherds on that night is announced to all of us, 'You will find a baby wrapped in swaddling clothes and lying in a manger.' We are all invited to gather around this child. There is something powerfully appealing about every newborn child. We are drawn to this bundle of vulnerable and amazing new life. We gather around in awe and wonder. We gather around the child of Mary and Joseph with an even greater sense of wonder. We are invited to find

God in this child, to come close to God as we would to a child. This child is the human face of God. Here is Emmanuel, God with us. God has become flesh in this newborn infant. God has come among us in this amazing way to welcome us. We are all welcome to gather around this child, the son of Mary and Joseph who is also the Son of God. God has become accessible to us through this vulnerable child who went on to become a vulnerable adult on a Roman cross. The wood of the manger and the wood of the cross both speak to us of God's desire to embrace us in his love. They both proclaim that God's light shines in our darkness and God's deeply personal love for each of us never dies away. We are sent from this feast to reflect something of the light of this love to each other.

Christmas: Mass during the Day · *God's complete word*

Is 52:7-10; Heb 1:1-6; Jn 1:1-18

Words are particularly important at this time of the year, both the spoken and the written kind. This shows itself in our efforts to speak to those close to us who are away from us at this time. We make a special effort to speak with members of our families who are living abroad. We feel the need to speak with those who are dear to us even if we cannot see them face to face. The written word is also important at this time of the year. Even in this digital age, we continue to write Christmas cards and send them off to people with a written greeting, including people we may not see from one Christmas to the next. In various ways, we feel the need to connect with each other at this Christmas time; we sense a call to communicate with one another. Language is one of the primary ways that we communicate with each other. Words carry greater significance than is usual in these days and weeks.

Perhaps we attach so much significance to words at this time of the year because we appreciate that the deeper meaning of Christmas has everything to do with communication. The Gospel reading today puts it very simply but very profoundly, 'In the beginning was the Word and the Word was with God and the Word was God. The Word was made flesh, he lived among us, and we saw his glory.' We all struggle to express ourselves, whether in the spoken word or the written word. We often end up with the nagging feeling that we haven't said all we wanted to say or in the way we wanted to say it. We feel that there is a great deal more within us, in our minds and hearts, than we have managed to put into words. God, however, expresses himself fully and completely, so perfectly that the word God spoke was itself God. It was that perfect word that became flesh, a human person, whose name was Jesus. The most perfect and precious word that God spoke became a person. As a result, those who looked on the face of the newborn child of Mary and Joseph were looking on the face of God. That child was the complete self-communication of God. Here was a baby who was God's perfect word to us. That word of God would unfold itself in the life, death and Resurrection of this child. Christmas celebrates the good news that in Jesus, God spoke a complete word to us, a word that said all that God could possibly say in human language, a word that was the culmination of all the words that God had spoken before the birth of Jesus. As the beginning of today's second reading puts it, 'At various times in the past and in various different ways, God spoke to our ancestors through the prophets, but in our own time, the last days, he has spoken to us through his son.'

We all know from our own experience the power of words. We understand that words can have a power for good or for ill. They can heal or hurt. They can bring light or cast a shadow. They can energise people or drain them of life. In certain situations especially, we know that we have to be very careful about what we say and how we say it. The word that God spoke and that became a human person was the most life-affirming word that was ever spoken. It was a creative word, a word that brings life to everyone who receives it, a life that endures beyond this earthly life. There wasn't any hint of darkness in the word that God spoke and that took human flesh in the person of Jesus; it was full of light. It was light itself. In the words of the Gospel reading, 'the Word was the true light that enlightens everyone'. Those who open their minds and their hearts to this word are bathed in God's light, the light of God's love and God's truth. This was a word that was full of everything good; in the words of today's Gospel reading, it was 'full of grace and truth'. There was a wonderful abundance about this word.

We know from our own experience that the best of human language, the most profound of human words, take time to digest. We find ourselves going back to such words over and over again. This is supremely true of that word of God that became flesh in Jesus. We need to keep returning to it over and over again to receive from its fullness. Today's feast calls on us to keep returning to this rich word that God spoke and continues to speak to us, and to keep on receiving from its fullness so that we ourselves can become fully mature with the fullness of Christ himself. Saint Ephrem, a fourth-century poet and theologian from the Syriac-speaking church wrote, 'God has fashioned his word with many beautiful forms, so that each one who studies it may consider what they like. He has hidden in his word all kinds of treasures so that each one of us, wherever we meditate, may be enriched by it.'

The Holy Family   *Becoming family*

Gn 15:1–6; 21:1–3; Heb 11:8, 11–12, 17–19; Lk 2:22–40

We have just celebrated the feast of Christmas. For most of us it is a time when we connect with the members of our family. At least for Christmas dinner we try to gather as family. Because family is important to us around Christmas time, we tend to feel the absence of family members more intensely at this time of the year. Christmas can be a very difficult time for those who have been recently bereaved. Our experience of family changes over the years. For those who get married and start a family of their own, their new family becomes more significant over time than their family of origin, especially as siblings move away and start families of their own. For those who do not get married and remain single, their family of origin tends to retains its power. Brothers and sisters can become important, especially after parents have died.

Throughout our lives, whether we are married or single, family remains important to us. The experience of family will differ for each of us. None of us has had a completely positive experience of family. As well as being places of warmth, love and support, our families can also be places of conflict, suffering and anguish. Yet, even the negative experience of family does not completely break the bond that we feel with family members. The family is such a fundamental human experience from which we can never completely break free, and, hopefully, most of us would not want to. Pope Francis said that all of humanity passes through the family. To that extent, the health of humanity is greatly dependant on the health of the family. At its best, the family is a communion of love, created by the loving commitment of a husband and wife to each other all the days of their lives.

Today's Feast of the Holy Family reminds us that Jesus was born into a family. The word became flesh as a member of a family, a family that included not just parents, but grandparents, aunts, uncles and cousins. At the end of today's Gospel reading, it is said that within his family in Nazareth of Galilee the child Jesus grew to maturity, and was filled with wisdom and God's favour was with him. Three elements are mentioned there which give us a lovely description of family life at its best: maturity, wisdom and God's favour. The family provides us with an environment where we can grow to maturity, not just physically, but emotionally, intellectually, spiritually, relationally. It is a place where we imbibe some of the wisdom we need to negotiate the journey of life. There is a great emphasis on knowledge today, and rightly so. Knowledge of all sorts is so much more accessible than it used to be. Yet, more fundamental than knowledge is wisdom, that quality which allows us to discern what is good, right, noble, true and loving, and then to act accordingly. Within his family in Nazareth, Jesus grew to maturity and was filled with wisdom. His family was also the place where God's favour rested on him. At its best, our family is a place where we experience something of God's loving favour. We speak of marriage as a sacrament. The love of husband and wife makes present the love of Christ for his church, the love of God for all humanity. The experience of family is our best opportunity to be graced by God's loving favour for us in Christ. It is there that we can experience in concrete ways something of the Lord's faithful love, his willingness to forgive us when we fail, to support us when we are at our most vulnerable.

We don't know much about the thirty years that Jesus spent with his family in Nazareth; they are the hidden years. Yet, without that experience of family, Jesus would not have become the adult that graces the pages of the Gospels, that fully mature human being, filled with wisdom, on whom God's favour rested and who revealed God's favour to all, especially to those who were made to feel outside of God's favour. Although Jesus was more than Mary and Joseph could ever give him, their influence on him can never be underestimated. They brought him to the point where one day he could separate himself from his blood family and begin to form a family of his own, not a blood family but a family of disciples, the family of those who do the will of his father in heaven. This family came to be called the Church, into which we have all been baptised.

There are three generations of people in today's Gospel reading. As well as the child Jesus and his young parents, there is the elderly Simeon and Anna. The gift that these two older people bring to this young married couple and their child is their ability to see and name the goodness of the child. Simeon declares him to be a light to enlighten the pagans and the glory of Israel; Anna announces that he will respond to people's longing for deliverance. Those of an older generation always have a gift to offer us that no one else can give. At its best, family life is where the different generations are brought together in ways that are deeply enriching for all.

Solemnity of Mary, Mother of God   *Pondering our faith*

Gn 15:1-6; 21:1-3; Heb 11:8, 11-12, 17-19; Lk 2:22-40

New Year's Day will always have special resonances for all of us. It is a day when we may find ourselves looking back over the year that has just gone. When we think back on that year we will all have our own memories. Some of them may be happy and others sad. New Year's Day is also a day when we look ahead to the year that is before us. We may be conscious of certain things that we would like to do differently to how we did them last year. We may find ourselves setting some goals that we would like to follow through on. In all kinds of ways, New Year's Day can be a reflective time. It can be a time to take stock, to look back on where we have been and to look forward to where we would like to be.

New Year's Day also encourages us to be reflective about our faith, about the Lord and his place in our lives. It is a day to ask, 'How can I grow in my relationship with the Lord? How can I respond more generously to his call? How might I find ways to nurture my faith or to live it more fully, more courageously?' Every so often we need to become more reflective about our relationship with the Lord, and how it is impacting on our day to day lives. New Year's Day is a good time for such reflection.

Today's Gospel reading presents Mary as a very reflective woman. We are told there that the shepherds went to Bethlehem and announced to all, including Mary, the message the angels had given them, which was, 'Do not be afraid ... I am bringing you good news of great joy for all the people: to you is born this day in the city of David a saviour who is Christ, the Lord.' The shepherds are the first human agents to proclaim the Gospel and the first to hear it from them are Mary and all who were with her. According to the Gospel reading, Mary's response to the shepherd's word was a contemplative one. 'She treasured all these things and pondered them in her heart.' It was as if there was too much in what the shepherds said to take in at once. The shepherds were conveying to Mary that her child was none other than the long-awaited Jewish Messiah, whose other titles were 'Saviour' and 'Lord'. Here was good news of great joy, not just for Mary but for all the people. There was much to ponder there, a great deal to treasure. At the very beginning of his Gospel, Luke is presenting Mary as a reflective, thoughtful, contemplative woman. Indeed, a little further on in that same chapter, Luke describes her in a very similar way. When the boy Jesus went missing in Jerusalem and his parents, after much searching, eventually found him, he said to them, 'Why were you searching for me? Did you not know that I must be in my Father's house?' In response to those questions of Jesus, Luke tells us that Mary and Joseph 'did not understand what he said to them' and that 'his mother treasured all these things in her heart'. Once again there was much to ponder upon in what Jesus said. The meaning of his words was not immediately clear. Just as in the case of the words of the angels to the shepherds, the words of Jesus to his parents needed to be mulled over and reflected upon.

When it comes to the Lord and his relationship with us and ours with him, there is always a great deal to ponder, to reflect upon, to treasure in our hearts. Reading the Gospels, for example, is not just like reading any other book. Because the Gospels are God's words in human words, there is a depth to them that cries out to be explored. The word of God can speak to us in all kinds of different ways. The same passage of scripture may speak to us in one way at one time and in another way at another time. It is the Lord who speaks to us through the scriptures and the Lord has different things to say to us at different times. The portrayal of Mary in today's Gospel reading encourages us to keep pondering the word, to keep treasuring it in our hearts. In that sense, we are all called to be contemplatives. Like

Mary, we try to dispose ourselves to hearing what the Lord is saying to us as we go through life. Yes, our faith shows itself in good works of all kinds, but there is that other, reflective, dimension to our faith, to our relationship with the Lord, as well. Saint Thérèse of Lisieux wrote in her autobiography, 'Above all, it is the Gospels that occupy my mind. I'm always finding fresh light there.' If we ponder and treasure the word like Mary, we too will find fresh light there. A saying attributed to a well-known baseball player in the United States captures this contemplative attitude. He said on one occasion, 'Sometimes I just sits and thinks, and then, sometimes I just sits.' Perhaps a resolution for the year ahead might be to create a space in our lives for a deeper encounter with the Lord.

Second Sunday after Christmas   *Shining like the sun*

Eccl 24:1-2, 8-12; Eph 1:3-6, 15-18; Jn 1:1-18

I rather like this time of year immediately after Christmas, because I know that the days are finally getting longer, even if it is not all that apparent. In terms of daylight hours, nothing much seems to have changed since well before Christmas. Yet, we know that from 21 December onwards, the light which has been retreating since late June, the longest day of the year, is now beginning its fight back, and that each day is that tiny bit longer than the previous day. The realisation that light is on the increase can lift our spirits. We sense that we have turned the corner and we begin to look ahead towards brighter days and longer evenings. Soon, with the increasing light, there will be increasing life in our gardens, as the very early flowers of spring begin to show their heads. Light and life tend to go together.

The Gospel reading today seems to be in harmony with this emergence of light in the natural world. It speaks of the Word that is the true light, a light that shines in the darkness, a light that darkness cannot overpower, a light that enlightens all people. This word who was the true light became flesh and dwelt among us. Later in John's Gospel Jesus will say of himself, 'I am the light of the world, whoever follows me will never walk in darkness but will have the light of life.' Christmas has often been called the Feast of Light. It celebrates the coming of God's light in the form of a human life, the life of Jesus. Perhaps this is why we light candles at this time of the year and decorate trees with bright lights. At some level, we recognise that we are celebrating the feast of a glorious light.

We have all known dark times. Many of us will have struggled with a darkness of spirit, for a whole variety of reasons. Some paths we have taken may not have led where we had hoped it would lead. A relationship that was once important to us may have died away. Some profound loss may have taken the heart out of us. An experience of failure of some kind deeply undermined our sense of self-worth. It is above all at such times that we need to hear afresh those words in today's Gospel reading about the true light that enlightens everyone, that shines in the dark and that darkness cannot overpower. This is not a distant light, like a distant star, which requires a sophisticated telescope to even glimpse. No, it is a light that shines from within our human experience, because the word who was the true light became flesh. He entered fully in every aspect of human life, including its darkest recesses, and shone a powerful light there, the light of God's presence, the light of God's love, of God's life. Today's Gospel reading proclaims that there is a life-giving light at the core of all human life, even in the darkest and most unpromising of our experiences. The Evangelist declares there that he has come to see this divine light above all in the human flesh of God's son. Speaking on behalf of the community of faith to which he belongs, he says, 'We have seen his glory, the glory that is his as the only son of the Father, full of grace and truth.'

This light which shines so brilliantly in the life, death and Resurrection of Jesus has cast its light upon all flesh and continues to shine from within all flesh. What we need are the eyes to see that divine light within us and around us, the presence of the light of the world. Thomas Merton was a Trappist monk and mystic whose writings have nourished the faith life of large numbers of men and women of our time. He once wrote about an experience he had as he sat on a bench in the town square, not far from his monastery. As he looked out upon the people of Louisville, Kentucky, coming and going, he saw them in a way he had never seen them before. He suddenly realised, 'It is a glorious destiny to be a member of the human race though it makes many terrible mistakes ... and yet God himself glories in becoming a member of it ... it was as if I suddenly saw the secret beauty of their hearts, where neither sin or shadow can reach, the core of their reality, the person that each one is in God's eyes. If only they could see themselves as they really are. Who will tell them that they are all walking around, shining like the sun?' Merton realised that these people going about their lives were no less graced, no less enlightened, than his brothers back in the monastery. Because of the word becoming flesh and dwelling among us, all of our lives are bathed in God's light, that true light which, in becoming flesh, enlightens all people. The Gospel reading promises us that if we welcome that light into our lives we will be empowered to become children of God; we will come to share in Jesus' own intimate relationship with God.

The Epiphany of the Lord   *Searching for a greater light*

Is 60:1-6; Eph 3:2-3, 5-6; Mt 2:1-12

The story of the magi from the East that we have just heard has inspired artists and poets down through the centuries. In the last century, the poet TS Eliot wrote a poem entitled, 'The Journey of the Magi', in which he describes a journey at the 'worst time of the year', the 'very dead of winter'. We celebrate this feast in the very dead of winter, when the days are short and dark. Yet the feast of the Epiphany is very much a feast of light. The word 'epiphany' means 'manifestation' or 'showing forth'. Today's feast celebrates the shining forth of Emmanuel, God with us, to all who are seeking the face of God, who are searching for truth, looking for meaning and purpose in their lives. The feast of the Epiphany announces that the Christ child is the journey's end for all such seekers.

The magi from the East are patrons of all who are searching for a greater light and a fuller truth. They are symbols of hope for all who struggle to God by strange routes. The writer Evelyn Waugh wrote a prayer to the magi for one of his fictional characters which catches something of this hope: 'You are my especial patrons, and patrons of all latecomers, of all who have a tedious journey to make to the truth, of all who are confused with knowledge and speculation.' It is likely that by using the term 'magi' Matthew intended scholars who studied the stars, and who, in contemplating the heavens, sought the God of heaven and earth. They hoped that the language of the stars would speak to them of God. When one unusual star appeared, they followed it, believing it would lead them to a newborn child who was the long-awaited King of the Jews, God's anointed one. Their journey was driven by a question, which they put to the inhabitants of Jerusalem on arriving in that great city, 'Where is the infant king of the Jews?' Often it is our questions that bring us closer to the Lord. The question 'Where is Jesus to be found?' is one of the deeper questions of life. People have always asked that question. They may not ask it in that form, but they ask, 'Where is truth to be found?' 'Where is light and life to be found?' They are, in reality, seeking the one who said of himself, 'I am the truth; I am the light; I am the life.' The magi are their patrons. They are patrons of us all because we all remain seekers until that day when we pass over from this life and come to see the Lord face to face. As St Augustine said, 'Our hearts are restless, until they rest in God.'

The magi were led to Bethlehem by a star. There is always a star that guides us towards Bethlehem. The Lord will find ways of drawing us towards himself, if we are genuinely searching for him. The Lord drew the magi to himself from within their own experience; they were stargazers and it was through the stars that he spoke to them. The Lord will speak to us too from within our experiences, if we have ears to hear. Yet, as the Lord draws us towards himself, there will be other forces that seek to draw us away from the Lord. The magi discovered this for themselves. As they came closer to their destination, they encountered people who were not genuine seekers after truth, Herod, the representative of the political power, and his allies, the chief priests and scribes. When Herod asked, 'Where is Jesus to be found?' where the King of the Jews was to be born, it was out of fear that here was someone who might threaten his own status as King of the Jews. His hypocrisy is evident is his invitation to the magi to return to him and tell him all about the child so that he may worship him. On our journey towards the Lord, we will inevitably encounter our own version of Herod and his entourage. That is why Jesus teaches us to pray, 'Lead us not into temptation, but deliver us from evil.'

When these strangers from the East finally reached the child whom they had been seeking, they worshipped him, and they placed at his service their most valuable treasures. They invite us to ask of ourselves,

'Before whom do we kneel in worship? Do we live worshipping the child of Bethlehem? Do we place at his feet our own possessions, our resources and gifts?' It is said of the magi that, having encountered the child, they returned to their country by a different way. The treasure they received from this child was more precious than the gifts they brought and it changed their lives forever; they went home different people. Any genuine encounter with the Lord will always change us in some fundamental way. The conclusion of Eliot's poem captures this truth, 'We returned to our places, these kingdoms, But no longer at ease here, in the old dispensation, With an alien people clutching their gods.'

The Baptism of the Lord   *The grace and call of Baptism*

Is 55:1-11; 1 Jn 5:1-9; Mk 1:7-11

Some of us may be able to look back over our lives and point to key moments that marked a significantly new phase on our life journey. It might be the day we met someone who went on to become a very important person in our life. It might be the time when we came to some place and we knew that this was the place for which we had been searching for many years. It might be the moment when we took on some task that would become hugely significant in shaping the kind of person we would become.

If Jesus were to have looked back over his life, he would probably point to his Baptism as the day that marked a significantly new phase in his life journey. Prior to his Baptism, he had lived a somewhat hidden life among his family and neighbours in Nazareth. After his Baptism, he set out on a very public mission that would take him far beyond Nazareth. That mission was to touch the lives of many of his contemporaries and, indeed, the lives of people all over the world in every succeeding generation. It was a mission that would cost him not less than everything. Even though Jesus was already thirty years of age at the time of his Baptism and, in effect, coming to the end of his relatively short life, the day of his Baptism was a hugely significant new beginning for him. According to today's Gospel reading, after his Baptism, Jesus experienced the coming of the Holy Spirit and a powerful assurance of God's favour, 'You are my son, the Beloved, my favour rests on you.' Graced in this way by the Holy Spirit and his father's word, he set out on the most important journey of his life.

Looking back over our lives, we might find it hard to think of our Baptism as marking a new beginning in our lives. Most of us were baptised shortly after birth and we would find it difficult to think of a time in our lives before Baptism. Yet, the fact that we were baptised so young does not make the day of our Baptism any less significant. On the day of our Baptism, something happened to us that shaped us for the rest of our lives, even though we had no awareness at the time. We cannot really answer the question 'Who am I?' without some reference to our Baptism. Christ was baptised not because he needed to repent of anything but to identify fully with God's people. He went down into the water with them. When we were baptised, we were identifying ourselves with Christ, or our parents were doing that on our behalf. From that day on, our identity was intimately linked with Christ's identity. We were baptised into him, sealed at the very core of our being with his spirit. To that extent, the day of our Baptism was a true watershed, a significant new beginning.

We are living in a much more multicultural Ireland than even fifteen or twenty years ago. The likelihood is that we will become even more multicultural in the years ahead. A growing number of people of other religions are coming to live among us. There is nothing to be lamented in this development. On the contrary, diversity, including religious diversity, has the potential to be very enriching for us all. One of the ways that this new religious diversity impacts on us as Christians, as Roman Catholics, is that it can raise more sharply for us the question of our baptismal identity. As we meet more and more people who are not baptised, we may be prompted to explore more fully the meaning of our own Baptism, and to ask ourselves, 'What does it mean for me to say: "I am baptised"'. When everyone else in our society was baptised, perhaps we did not feel the same need to ask this question.

To say to ourselves or to others, 'I am baptised', is to make a statement that is rich in meaning. What our Baptism means for us bears some relationship to what Jesus' Baptism meant for him. At our Baptism, the Holy Spirit came down upon us, as it came down upon him. At our Baptism God, our heavenly father, said to us what was said to Jesus at his Baptism: 'You are my son, my daughter, the beloved; my favour rests on you.' When we were baptised, we were graced, like Jesus, with the gift of the Holy Spirit and the assurance of God's favour. What God said to us on the day of our Baptism, he says to us every day of our lives. The gift of the Spirit God gave us then, God renews each day. That is why we say, 'I am baptised', rather than 'I was baptised'. Alongside this grace of Baptism goes the call of Baptism. Like Jesus, having been graced, we are sent forth to live out of the grace that we have received. Having been christened, we are called to live Christ-like lives. Having been baptised into Christ, we are called to allow Christ to live in and through us. Each day we try to discern what that means for us in the concrete circumstances of our own day-to-day lives.

LENT

First Sunday of Lent   *Wild beasts and angels*

Gn 9:8-15; 1 Pt 3:18-22; Mk 1:12-15

This is the first Sunday of Lent. The word 'Lent' comes from an Anglo-Saxon word meaning 'springtime' and the season of Lent came to be associated with the springtime of our souls. The season of spring has begun in nature; we are becoming aware of the first signs of growth. In harmony with nature, Lent is that season in the Church when we are called to grow spiritually, to grow in our relationship with the Lord, with each other and with the earth in which we live. It is a time for us to stand still, and to take a moment to decide who we are and what it is we want to do in the world for and with others and in honour of the God who created us. If that sounds like what we would normally do when we are on retreat, Lent is a kind of retreat. It is a time when the whole Church is called to go on retreat for a period of about five weeks. We engage in this time of retreat with other believers, as a church. Together we step back and invite the Lord to help us refocus our lives so that at the end of Lent, on Easter Sunday, we can renew our baptismal promises with conviction and recommit ourselves to the way of life that our Baptism has called us to take.

Our forty days of Lent is an echo of the forty days that Jesus spent in the wilderness immediately after his Baptism. This was his time of retreat, during which he stood back and asked himself who he was and what he was to do in the world with and for others and in honour of God his father. It was his time to enter fully into the Baptism he had just received. This year we read Mark's version of Jesus' forty days in the wilderness. Mark simply says that Jesus remained in the wilderness for forty days where he was tempted by Satan; he was with the wild beasts and the angels looked after him. During a time of retreat, we often come to see more clearly what is going on in our lives at that deeper level that we are not always aware of in the midst of our normal daily routine. The Gospel reading suggests that during his time of retreat, Jesus become more aware of those two fundamental realities that would be present to him throughout his ministry: the wild beasts and the angels. The wild beasts were those forces that were opposed to who he was and to all that he was sent into the world to do; Jesus understood these wild beasts to be the agents of Satan. The angels are the expression of the nearness of God who would take care of Jesus and protect him and his mission. God's comforting and empowering presence would often express itself in and through other people. At the beginning of his Gospel Mark says that when Jesus was in the wilderness 'angels looked after him'. Then at the end of his Gospel, at the very moment when Jesus dies, Mark refers to the women at the foot of the cross and says of them that they used to 'look after him while he was in Galilee'. These women were one expression of the angels, of God's comforting and protective presence. The wild beasts, those forces that tried to prevent Jesus from being true to his baptismal calling, found expression in the religious leaders who opposed him from early on, the political leaders who crucified him and, even at times, Jesus' own disciples. On one occasion, Jesus said to Peter, 'Get behind me Satan', when Peter rebuked Jesus for speaking about his coming suffering and death.

Insofar as we enter into our own lenten retreat, we too will become aware of these same two fundamental realities, the wild beasts and the angels. We can probably all identify those influences that put our faith to the test, that undermine our relationship with the Lord, that threaten our baptismal identity as temples of the Holy Spirit, members of Christ's body, sons and daughters of God. These influences lead us into ways of thinking, relating and behaving that are not inspired by the Gospel, that are not expressions of that kingdom of God that Jesus proclaims in today's Gospel reading. However, we will also become aware, as we enter our Lenten retreat, of the presence of the angels, those many manifestations of God's caring and supportive presence that enable us to claim our baptismal identity more fully and live it more completely. We are surrounded by wonderful resources that God has placed at our disposal – the word of God, the sacraments, the community of faith. As Jesus says in the opening message of his ministry in today's Gospel reading, 'the kingdom of God is at hand'. God's empowering presence is at hand now for all of us and God's power working on our behalf is stronger than the forces that work against God's purpose for our lives. That is why in our struggle to be faithful to our baptismal calling, we should never lose heart. We always face the powers that are opposed to the Gospel in the company of the Lord and the various angels he places at our disposal.

Second Sunday of Lent   *Freedom to let go*

Gn 22:1-2, 9-13, 15-18; Rm 8:31-34; Mk 9:2-10

I came across a sentence in a book I was reading recently which struck me very forcibly: 'All love relationships flourish only when there is freedom to let go of what is precious, so as to receive it back as a gift.' It is not easy to let go of what is precious. The more precious someone is to us, the harder it is to let go of that person. The more attractive someone is to us, the more we feel inclined to possess that person. Yet, in the effort to possess someone we can easily lose them. At the heart of all loving relationships is the freedom to let go of the other, and in letting go, to receive the other back as a gift. Parents know that there comes a time when they have to let go of their sons or daughters, even though they are more precious to them than anything else. They may have to let them go to another country or to the person whom they have chosen as their future spouse. Yet, in letting go of their children, parents invariably discover that they receive them back as a gift. Single people too have to learn the freedom of letting go what is precious so as to receive it back as a gift. In any good and healthy friendship, people need to give each other plenty of space.

In today's first reading, Abraham is portrayed as being willing to let go of what was most precious to him, the only son of his old age. In being willing to let his son go to God, he went on to receive him back as a gift. Many people find it a very disturbing story, because it portrays God as asking Abraham to sacrifice his only beloved son as a burnt offering to God. We are rightly shocked by the image of God asking a father to sacrifice his son in this way. Abraham lived about a thousand years before Christ. In the religious culture of that time it was not uncommon for people to sacrifice their children to various gods. The point of the story seems to be that the God of Israel is not like the pagan gods. If Abraham thought that God was asking him to sacrifice his son Isaac, like the people who worshipped other gods, he was wrong. God was not asking this of Abraham. Yet, the willingness of Abraham to let go of what was most precious to him if that was what God was asking remained an inspiration to the people of Israel. He had already shown a willingness to let go of his family and his homeland as he set out towards an unknown land in response to God's call.

The Early Church came to understand the relationship between Abraham and Isaac as pointing ahead to the relationship between God the Father and Jesus. Like Abraham, God was prepared to let go of what was most precious to him, his one and only son, out of love for humanity. God was prepared to let his son go to humanity, with all the dangers that entailed for his son. Saint Paul was very struck by this extraordinary generosity of God on our behalf, as he says in today's second reading, 'God did not spare his own son, but gave him up to benefit us all.' God let his precious son go to humanity even though the consequences of that were the rejection of his son and, ultimately, his crucifixion. Even after Jesus was crucified, God continued to give him to us as risen Lord. When Paul contemplates this self-emptying love of God for us, he asks aloud, in the opening line of that second reading, 'With God on our side who can be against us?' Paul is declaring that if God's love for us is this complete, then we have nothing to fear from anyone. Here is a love that has no trace of possessiveness, a love that makes us lovable.

In today's Gospel reading, Peter, James and John are taken by Jesus up a high mountain, and there they have an experience of Jesus which took their breath away, an experience that was so precious that Peter could not let it go. He wanted to prolong it indefinitely and so he says to Jesus, 'Rabbi, it is wonderful for us to be here, so let us make three tents, one for you, one for Moses and one for Elijah.' He and the other two disciples had a fleeting glimpse of the heavenly beauty of Christ, and did not want to let go of it. Beauty always attracts; it calls out to us. Yet, Peter and the others had to let go of this precious experience; it was only ever intended to be momentary. They would receive it back in the next life as a gift. For now, their task was to listen to Jesus, 'This is my beloved son. Listen to him.' That is our task too. We spend our lives listening to the Lord as he speaks to us in his word and in the circumstances of our lives; we listen to him as a preparation for that wonderful moment when we see him face to face in eternity and we can finally say, 'it is wonderful to be here', without the need to let go.

Third Sunday of Lent

The Lord's purifying work

Ex 20:1-17; 1 Cor 1:22-25; Jn 2:13-25

Compared to earlier generations, one of the features that characterises this generation is speed. We can communicate with one another at a speed that would have been unthinkable a couple of generations ago. An email reaches its destination on the other side of the world in a matter of seconds. Journeys that took days or even weeks in the time of my grandparents now take hours. Builders build much faster than they built in the past. Many of us probably think that much of what has been built quickly may not endure; it won't stand the test of time.

In the ancient world, the world of Jesus, the world of the Early Church, buildings, especially significant political or religious buildings, were built to last. If you go to Rome today, you can still see the remains of the significant political and religious buildings of the Roman Empire. In Jerusalem, in the time of Jesus, the most significant public building by far was a religious building, the temple. In today's Gospel reading, the Jewish authorities remind Jesus that it had taken forty-six years to build the temple. Indeed, in the time of Jesus, the temple begun by Herod the Great was not yet complete. It would take another fourteen years, sixty years in all, for it to be finally finished. If a building firm gave a timescale of sixty years to complete a building today, it is fair to say that they would be unlikely to get the contract.

Jesus was aware of the huge religious and political significance of the temple in his day, and yet he challenged it, and he challenged those responsible for it, because he recognised that the temple was not in fact serving God's purposes. As Jesus says in today's Gospel reading, 'Stop turning my Father's house into a market.' There is a big difference between a house and a market. A house has the potential to be a home. A market could never really be a home; people go to markets to buy and sell. Buying and selling are not activities you associate with home. The temple was to be God's house, God's home, a place where all people could feel at home in God's presence. The activities associated with the market were preventing the temple from being the home that God wanted it to be, a spiritual home for all the nations. Jesus saw that here was an institution in need of reform.

Every institution, including every religious institution, is always in need of reform. The Church, in so far as it is a human institution, is in need of ongoing reform. The Church exists to serve the purposes of God, the purposes of God's son, in the world. However, inevitably, because the Church is composed of human beings, it can also serve as a block to God's purposes. The Church is called to be the sacrament of Christ, to reveal the powerful and life-giving presence of Christ to the world. However, invariably, it will often hide Christ or reveal a distorted image of Christ to the world, one that is not fully in keeping with the Gospels. In the second reading, Paul sets God's wisdom over against human wisdom, God's power over against human strength. The Church can sometimes substitute God's wisdom with human wisdom, God's power with human strength. Just as in the Gospel reading Jesus wanted to purify the temple, the risen Lord is constantly working to purify the Church. All of us who make up the Church need to be open to his purifying presence. In the words of the Book of Revelation, we need to be listening to what the Spirit, the Spirit of the risen Lord, is saying to us, the Church. Those in positions of leadership in the Church have a special responsibility to listen to what the Spirit may be saying to the Church, so as to bring it more into line with what God intends. However, we are all called to listen to the challenging word of the Spirit and to be open to the purifying presence of the risen Lord. We are all the Church, and we all have our part to play in ensuring that the Church is what the Lord intends it to be. Lent is a time when we try to listen to what the Spirit may be saying to us about our lives; it is a time when as individuals and as a community we are called to allow the Spirit to renew our lives so that we conform more fully to the image and likeness of Christ.

The fiery Jesus of the Gospel reading, who is passionate about what God wants, remains alive and active at the heart of the Church today. The relationship between the Lord and the Church, between the Lord and each one of us, will always be marked by a certain tension, because the Lord will always be working to purify and renew us. In the light of the Gospel reading we might ask ourselves in what ways we have allowed the values of the marketplace to override the values of the Gospel in our own lives, in the life of our society, in the life of our church.

Fourth Sunday of Lent

God's work of art

2 Chr 36:14-16, 19-23; Eph 2:4-10; Jn 3:14-21

A painting hung for many years on a dining room wall in a Jesuit house in Dublin. No one paid much attention to it until one day someone with a keen eye realised that this could be something of great value. It was further investigated by art experts, and it turned out that this painting was the work of the great Italian artist Caravaggio. The painting of the arrest of Jesus is now one of the National Gallery's great treasures. All those years it had hung in the dining room of Lesson Street it was no less a treasure, but its value went unrecognised. It hung there waiting to be discovered, waiting for someone to recognise its true value as a work of art.

According to the letter to the Ephesians we read from this evening, we are all 'God's work of art, created in Christ Jesus to live the good life'. We don't tend to think of ourselves as works of art. Yet, like the person who spotted the painting in Lesson Street, God knows our true worth, our true value. We are works of art to God; we are of great worth and value in God's sight.

We can all think of people in our own lives whom we value greatly, whose worth to us is beyond price, because to us they are works of art. When someone is a treasure to us, we don't count the cost in their regard. We will do anything we can for them. We will travel long distances to see them; we will stay up half the night to be with them if they are ill; we will protect them with all our passion when necessary. How we relate to those we value and treasure is not determined so much by how they relate to us. Even if they do something that annoys us, we tend to make all kinds of allowances for them. We say something like 'that's just the way he/she is'. Their worth in our eyes is rooted in something deeper than what they do or fail to do. We value them, simply, for who they are.

Our experience of how we relate to those we value, and of how people who value us relate to us, gives us a glimpse of how God relates to us. God loves us in a way that does not count the cost. The Gospel reading today expresses that truth very simply: 'God loved the world so much that he gave his only son.' God sent his son out of love for us and that sending became a giving when his son was put to death on a cross. Here was a love that did not count the cost, a sending that became a costly giving when that was called for. As Paul says in the second reading, 'God loved us so much that he was generous with his mercy.' We are of such value in God's eyes that God did not spare his own son, but gave him up to benefit us all. It is not surprising that the cross has become the dominant symbol of Christianity. This is not because we glorify suffering in any way, but because we recognise that the cross is a powerful sign of how much God values us, how precious we are in God's sight; it shows the extent to which God is prepared to go to express love for us.

Our love for those we value is bestowed on them for who they are more than for what they do. The same is true of God's love for us in Christ. As Paul says in the second reading, 'it is not based on anything you have done'. Some of us find it difficult to really believe that. We find ourselves asking, 'Have I done enough?' Yet, when it comes to someone in our lives whom we know truly loves us, we would never think of asking them, 'Have I done enough?' Why should we ask such a question of God, when even the greatest of human love only gives us a glimpse of God's love? God loves us for who we are, people made in the image of God's son, and, to that extent, works of art.

What God asks of us is that we receive God's love revealed and made present in Christ, or, in the words of the Gospel reading today, that we come into the light. The light of God's love falls upon us, but we can hide from it. Children fear the darkness very often. But as adults we often fear the light, because we suspect that the light will expose us in some way. Yet, the light of God is not a harsh light, the kind of light that is trained on a suspect in an interrogation room. It is a strong, yet warm light that brings healing and generates new life. It is an empowering light that enables us to 'live the good life', as Paul says in the second reading. As the hours of daylight are increasing in these days, we pray that the life-giving light of God's love will renew us and fill us with a new desire to serve him.

Fifth Sunday of Lent   *Coming to see Jesus*

Jer 31:31–4; Heb 5:7–9; Jn 12:20–30

We probably all have a wish list of things we would like to do before we die, or, perhaps people we would like to meet. If we were given a blank sheet of paper with the words 'I wish …' at the top and asked to fill it in, we would likely all come up with a different list, although there might be some elements in common. What we would have in common would probably be the more important, deeper realities of life, such as health, peace of mind, loving relationships, happiness for oneself and one's loved ones, a more just and peaceful world. As people of faith we might include on our blank page some expression of our religious longings. We might wish for a deeper experience of the Lord's love and forgiveness in our lives or for greater clarity as to what the Lord is asking of us or desires for us.

At the beginning of today's Gospel reading we are introduced to two people who approach one of the disciples of Jesus and express their wish in a very simple way, saying, 'We should like to see Jesus.' They are described as 'Greeks'. In saying to Philip, 'We want to see Jesus', they are giving expression to their deeper religious longings. No matter where we are on our own faith journey, there is a sense in which we can always say, 'we want to see Jesus'. Those two Greeks were at the very beginning of their faith journey as followers of Jesus. Yet, their wish is appropriate for every stage of the journey. When it comes to the Lord, there is always more to be seen. When it comes to our relationship with the Lord, there is always room for growth. Saint Paul was one of the few people in the New Testament who had seen the risen Lord. Writing to the church in Corinth, he says, 'Have I not seen Jesus our Lord?' Yet in that same letter, he acknowledges, 'For now, we see as in a mirror dimly; but then we will see face to face.' In that eternal moment beyond this earthly life we will see the Lord clearly, face to face. Now, we see dimly, and so we can always say, 'I want to see Jesus. I want to see him more clearly.' In his letter to the Philippians, Paul gives expression to this wish, this longing to see the Lord more clearly, when he says, 'I want to know Christ.' We might be tempted to say to him, 'Surely, you already know Christ.' He would reply to us, quoting again his first letter to the Corinthians, 'Now I know only in part; then I will know fully, even as I have been fully known.' It is only 'then' beyond this earthly life that we will know the Lord fully, will see him clearly. Until then, we are among the Greeks in today's Gospel reading who say, 'We want to see Jesus.'

It is striking that the two Greeks did not approach Jesus directly. They approached one of Jesus' disciples, Philip, and in turn went to Andrew and then, together, they went to Jesus with the request of the Greeks. The two disciples, Philip and Andrew, served as mediators between the Greeks and Jesus. These two disciples made it possible for the two Greeks to see Jesus. This is as true today as it was in the time of Jesus. We come to the Lord through each other. We are called to bring each other to the Lord, to help one another to see Jesus. In our faith life, in our search for Jesus, we are intimately bound up with one another. Parents help their children to see Jesus by teaching them to pray, bringing them to the church, reading passages from the Gospels to them. Children, in turn, can bring their parents, and all of us, to see Jesus. Their unselfconscious desire to know the Lord, their openness to prayer and the world of the spirit, can touch us deeply, and even awaken some faith in us that has been dormant for some time. When it comes to our faith, we are all struggling to see, we are all a little blind and we need others to show us and to guide us.

If at the beginning of today's Gospel reading we have two Greeks wanting to see Jesus, at the end of that reading we have those wonderful words of Jesus, 'When I am lifted up from the earth, I will draw all people to myself.' Jesus declares there that when he is lifted up on the cross and lifted up in glory, he will be revealing his love for us and that love will draw us to himself. The one whom we wish to see is not playing hide and seek with us. Rather, he is constantly drawing us to himself in love. He is the grain of wheat that falls into the earth and dies and in dying bears much fruit. His dying is an explosion of love that envelopes us and is constantly working to pass our wish to see him more clearly.

Palm Sunday *Looking upon the cross with eyes of faith*

Is 50:4-7; Phil 2:6-11; Mk 14:1-15:47

There is a very sharp contrast between the short Gospel we read at the beginning of Mass and the story of the passion and death of Jesus we have just heard. The crowd who cried 'Hosanna' as Jesus entered Jerusalem went on to cry 'crucify him'. Those who welcome him with great euphoria went on to jeer and mock him as he hung from a Roman cross. Why such a sudden change of attitude? When Jesus entered Jerusalem he was welcomed as one who would usher in the 'kingdom of our father David'. Here, it was believed, was the king who would restore the fortunes of King David and rid the land of Roman occupation. However, within the space of a week those expectations were shattered. Their king would end up on a Roman cross. Whereas people wanted victory, the cross spoke of defeat; whereas they looked for a power greater than Rome's, the cross spoke of weakness; whereas they had hoped for a wise leader, the cross spoke of foolishness; whereas they looked to Jesus to demonstrate God's powerful presence, the cross spoke of God's absence. The shattering of their expectations turned their jubilation into hostility.

Yet, there were a few people who saw the horror of Jesus' crucifixion with very different eyes to most of the people. A pagan soldier, the Roman centurion who looked on at how Jesus died, exclaimed, 'This man was a son of God.' A prominent member of the Jewish ruling council took the bold step of going to Pilate because he recognised that this man was worthy of a dignified burial, rather than being thrown into a common grave which was the normal fate of the crucified. The women disciples who looked on from a distance took note of where Jesus was buried and went away to prepare spices to anoint his body at the earliest opportunity. These two men, a pagan and a Jew, and this group of women saw with different eyes and behaved in a fashion that was noble and generous.

The story we have just heard invites us to identify with those who looked beneath the surface of the broken and bloodied body on the cross and glimpsed there something of God. When we look upon the cross with the eyes of faith, we see a divine love that is stronger than sin, a divine light that shines in all our darkness, a divine power that brings new life out of all our deaths, a divine poverty that enriches us at the deepest level of our being. We have just heard the story of Jesus' last journey in the space of ten minutes. This Holy Week, the Church invites us to travel that journey at a much slower pace, day by day as it were. This is a good week to read through Mark's account of Jesus' passion and death slowly and prayerfully, a little every day. As we read we are invited to enter into that journey with the eyes of faith, with the eyes of the centurion, of Joseph of Arimathea and of the women. We look beneath the surface of what is happening, we listen deeply to all that is taking place, so that we see and hear the God who so loved the world that he gave his only son so that we may have life and live it to the full.

SACRED
TRIDUUM

Holy Thursday

Ex 12:1-8, 11-14; 1 Cor 11:23-6; Jn 13:1-15

It is often the case that certain events, certain happenings, can only be understood in hindsight. At the time the event is taking place, when we are in the midst of it, we do not really understand what is going on. We need to move on from it and to look back on it to grasp what was really taking place. Hindsight gives us a perspective which is simply not possible to have at the time. In this evening's Gospel reading, having washed the feet of his disciples, Jesus declared to Peter, 'At the moment, you do not know what I am doing, but later you will understand.' At the time, Peter did not understand what Jesus was doing by washing his feet. That is why he objected so strongly to what was happening. It was only later, after the death and Resurrection of Jesus and the coming of the Holy Spirit, that Peter and the other disciples understood the true meaning of what Jesus was doing.

Peter's objection to Jesus washing his feet was understandable. In that culture only slaves washed the feet of guests, whereas the disciples recognised Jesus as their Master and their Lord. It was only after Jesus' death and Resurrection that they understood that in laying down his garments to wash their feet, Jesus was indicating in advance what he was about to do on the following afternoon. On the cross Jesus laid down his life for his disciples and for all of humanity. 'No one has greater love than this,' he had said, 'than to lay down one's life for one's friends.' In laying down his garments to wash the feet of his disciples, Jesus was anticipating that laying down of his life for them and for all of us on the following afternoon. The love which inspired Jesus to wash the feet of his disciples was the same love that he gave full expression to on the cross. In a similar way, when during the same meal Jesus took bread, blessed it, broke it and gave it to his disciples and when he took a cup of wine, blessed it and gave it to his disciples, saying, 'this is my body ... this is my blood', he anticipated that gift of his body and blood, that gift of himself, which he would make for all on the cross.

That same self-giving love of Jesus is present to us every time we gather to celebrate the Eucharist. That is why St Paul says at the end of this evening's second reading, 'Every time you eat this bread and drink this cup, you are proclaiming the Lord's death.' To proclaim the Lord's death is to proclaim the Lord's love which found expression in his willingness to lay down his life for us all. Saint Paul says in one of his letters, 'I live by faith in the Son of God who loved me and gave himself for me.' That is what we proclaim every time we celebrate the Eucharist. We proclaim the presence of the Lord 'who loved me and gave himself for me'. It is that self-giving love of Jesus that the disciples were experiencing when Jesus laid down his garments and bent down to wash their feet.

That is why Jesus was so insistent that Peter allow him to wash his feet, 'If I do not wash you, you can have nothing in common with me.' Peter, and the other disciples, had to learn to receive the Lord's love on his terms. Peter did not consider himself worthy to have his feet washed. Yet, Jesus does not ask us to be worthy of his love, but simply to receive it as a gift. He loves us in our unworthiness. As St Paul says in his letters to the Romans, 'While we were still sinners, Christ died for us.' On that night before he died, Jesus washed the feet of all his disciples, including the feet of Judas who was about to betray him. Even though he knew what Judas, was about to do, Jesus did not love him any less than he loved the other disciples. All that was asked of the disciples, including Judas, was to receive the gift of his love. Peter struggled to receive this gift; he initially refused to allow Jesus to wash his feet, but then he relented. Judas allowed Jesus to wash his feet but could not receive the love which that action expressed. Receiving love can be difficult for all of us, especially when we know that the love is undeserved. Yet, the call to receive the Lord's gift of himself is at the heart of our Christian calling. It is at the heart of this evening's celebration. We all desperately need the outpouring of the Lord's love which can wash away our sins. The good news is that this love is there for the asking; it is there for the receiving. Like Peter, we can struggle to receive the gift of his love. We might protest, 'not my feet, not me'. As in the case of Peter, the Lord will work on our resistance until we surrender to him and allow him to relate to us in the way he wants to relate to us. Only when we learn to receive his love will we really be free to live the Lord's new commandment, 'Love one another, as I have loved you'.

Good Friday

The completion of Jesus' work

Is 52:13–53:12; Heb 4:14–16; 5:7–9; Jn 18:1–19:42

Today is a very solemn day in the Church's calendar. It is the only day in the Church's year when Mass is not celebrated anywhere in the Church. There is a definite restraint about Good Friday. We are remembering the crucifixion of Jesus. That is why on this day and on no other day we gather at three o'clock in the afternoon, because according to the Gospels Jesus was crucified at that time. Jesus did not seek to be crucified. In the Garden of Gethsemane, he prayed that, if possible, he should be spared it. He did not want himself or anyone else to suffer. He spent his life fighting suffering and healing brokenness at every level: physical, moral and spiritual. He stood against everything that was destructive of human living. He came so that we may have life and have it to the full. That is why he healed the broken, forgave sinners, and sought out the lost.

It was Jesus' total dedication to his life-giving work which resulted in his being crucified. His work of love aroused the hostility of powerful people. He was including in his circle, in God's circle, those whom the religious leaders believed should be excluded if the law of God was to be respected. Yet, Jesus continued to do the work God had given him to do, even though it angered those who had the power and influence to have him put to death. He was crucified because he was faithful to God's work on behalf of all of us. His love for God and for all those to whom God sent him was so great that he was prepared to suffer the most shameful of deaths rather than betray that love in any way. His death on the cross was something he accepted rather than sought out. He willingly accepted the full force of human evil as the price of remaining faithful to what he had been engaged in all his life, the loving service of God and all of God's people.

In that sense, his death on the cross confirms what he stood for all his life, his proclamation of God's love for all, especially those who were made to feel excluded from God's love. Jesus' death was in perfect harmony with his life. Indeed, if his life proclaimed God's love for all, his death did so even more powerfully. If he spent his life doing God's good work, his death brought that work to completion. That is why in the story of his passion and death from John's Gospel that was just read we hear Jesus exclaim at the moment of his death, 'It is accomplished.' He was saying, 'My work is finished.'

It is because the cross of Jesus proclaims a love greater than any human love, a divine love, that we venerate the cross, on this day above all days. In approaching the cross this afternoon, we know that we are approaching the throne of God's gracious love. We draw near to the cross with the conviction of St Paul when he says in his letter to the Galatians, 'I live by faith in the Son of God who loved me and gave himself for me'. Our veneration of the cross is our way of expressing our gratitude for the incredible love of God revealed in Jesus' life, death and Resurrection, a love that is stronger than human sin.

As we venerate the cross, we invite the Lord to continue his life-giving work through us. We commit ourselves again to becoming channels of his love to others. In venerating the wood of the Lord's cross, we also promise to venerate and respond to his presence in the sufferings of others. On this Good Friday, as we venerate the one who suffered and was broken on our behalf, we renew our desire to share in his work of fighting suffering and healing brokenness.

Easter Vigil

Surprised by joy

Rm 6:3-11; Mk 16:1-7

Most of the time, our lives follow a certain routine. We more or less know what to expect each day. The details may change but the pattern generally remains much the same. Every so often, however, something comes along that is completely unexpected. Our day takes a surprising turn. Sometimes the nature of the surprise can be unpleasant. At other times the surprise can be delightful. In the words of the title of a book written by C.S. Lewis, we can find ourselves 'surprised by joy'.

The title of that book is a good description of the experience of Jesus' disciples on the first Easter morning. The Gospel narratives suggest that the discovery of Jesus' empty tomb came as a complete surprise to the women who were the first to the empty tomb. The empty tomb of Jesus just was not part of the expected script. The empty tomb spoke volumes although its full meaning was not immediately understood by the women. The real meaning of the empty tomb was that, in the words of today's Gospel reading, the crucified one 'has risen, he is not here'. The emptiness of the tomb proclaimed that Jesus had passed over into a fullness of new life. The realm of death had been emptied of its power. The empty tomb announced that love, not hatred and prejudice, had won the day, the love of Jesus for God the Father and for all of us and the love of God for his son. The women who came to the tomb discovered that Jesus was not dead but was living among them in a way that transcended all their hopes and expectations. Whereas the passion and death of Jesus is very much about the work of men, in the Gospel stories of the finding of the empty tomb it is the women who are to the fore. It is the women who are entrusted with the good news that Jesus has risen. As in so many other contexts, it is the women who emerge as the protectors and guardians of unexpected new life.

The Resurrection of Jesus defies explanation. It does not lend itself easily to rational analysis. The Gospel stories tell us that when the women went to the other disciples to proclaim the good news that the tomb was empty and that Jesus had been raised from the dead, the other disciples did not believe their story. They had to go to the tomb for themselves. They could not bring themselves to believe such staggering news. We often say of something that 'it is too good to be true'. That seems to have been the view of the disciples on that first Easter morning. Sometimes we can be ready to believe anything but good news. Tonight, we are all being asked to renew our faith in the good news that the one who was crucified in weakness has risen in power. His bones are not to be found in any tomb in Jerusalem.

Where then is he to be found? He is to be found among us all; he lives in a special way within the believing community, which is his body. What Paul said to the church in Corinth, he would say to all of us gathered in this church tonight, 'Now you are the body of Christ, and individually members of it.' Within the believing community, the risen Lord is present to us in a privileged way in and through the Eucharist. In that same first letter to the Corinthians, Paul asks, 'the cup of blessing that we bless, is it not a communion in the blood of Christ? The bread that we break is it not a communion in the body of Christ?' Like the first disciples in the days after Jesus' Resurrection, we continue to recognise the Lord in the breaking of bread. Without the Resurrection, there would have been no church and no Eucharist; there would have been no written Gospels. As Paul says in that same first letter to the Corinthians, 'If Christ has not been raised, then our proclamation has been in vain and your faith has been in vain.'

We don't just celebrate Easter on Easter Sunday. We celebrate Easter every day, because every day the Lord is risen. Every day the risen Lord works among us and within us, working to raise us up from falsehood to truth, from despondency to hope, from hatred to love, from death to new life. In whatever darkness we may find ourselves, we always dwell in the light of Easter. When the women came to the empty tomb, the message they received was the risen Lord 'is going before you to Galilee'. The same risen Lord goes before his disciples in every age, raising us from our own tombs, whether it be the tombs we have built for ourselves or the tombs others have built for us. The risen Lord always goes before us because, in the words of St Patrick's Breastplate, he is with us, within us, behind us, before us, beside us. Easter is an everyday feast and we are always an Easter people. Even as we struggle with our own Good Fridays, the light and power of the risen Lord continues to envelope us, which is why we can all make our own those words of Paul, 'I can do all things in him who gives me strength.'

EASTER

Easter Sunday Morning *Creating a culture of life*

Acts 10:34, 37-43; Col 3:1-4; Jn 20:1-9

We are all only too well aware of the reality of death. We hear almost every day of those killed on our roads, mothers, fathers, teenagers and children. We are horrified at the number of people who are being callously murdered in our country. Some people in this church may have had their own very personal experience of death during the last year, with the loss of a loved one. From time to time we are reminded of our own mortality when we brush up against serious illness.

When Mary Magdalene approached the tomb of Jesus on that first Easter morning, she was preoccupied with death. Jesus, whose healing love she had experienced, had been cruelly put to death by the Romans in his prime. She had stood by the cross and watched him die. Now she was approaching the tomb to complete the rituals associated with death, by anointing Jesus' body with oils and perfumes. To her amazement, she discovered the tomb was empty. This discovery only added to her darkness of spirit, her grief. Not only had Jesus been put to death, but his body had been stolen. It was only when the risen Jesus appeared to her and called her by name that she understood why the tomb was empty. The tomb was empty because Jesus had been raised from the dead and was now alive. Filled with new joy, new hope, new energy, she went to the disciples and excitedly declared, 'I have seen the Lord.'

That declaration of Mary Magdalene, 'I have seen the Lord', is the heart of the Easter message. Jesus who was crucified has been raised by the Father and has been given the name 'Lord' which is above all names. Easter declares that the one we worship is a living Lord. The good news of Easter is that the tomb of death has been transformed by God into the womb of new life. This took everyone by surprise. The Gospel reading suggests that even Peter did not immediately understand the true meaning of the empty tomb. It is only of the beloved disciple that the Evangelist says: 'He saw and believed.' He alone understood why the tomb was empty; he alone saw that life had triumphed over death. Even before the risen Lord appeared to him, he understood that Jesus was risen. There will always be some who see more deeply than others.

The feast of Easter is the feast of life. In a culture where death can be so dominant, we need to savour this feast of life. At Easter, we renew our faith in a living God who brings new life out of death. If the death of Jesus reveals a God of love, the Resurrection of Jesus reveals a God of life. We know from our own experience that genuine human love is always life-giving, and divine love is profoundly life-giving. At Easter, we celebrate not only what the God of life has done for Jesus, but what God can do for us all. Because of Easter, we can face our own personal death with hope. Easter teaches us that the journey to the tomb is not ultimately a journey to death but, rather, as Mary Magdalene discovered, a journey to a wonderful and surprising new life. In the face of death, we too, like her, will discover that 'no eye has seen, nor ear heard, nor the human heart conceived what God has prepared for those who love him'.

If Easter enables us to face our own death with hope, it also encourages us to look at all our other experiences of death with new eyes. There is a sense in which we must deal with death throughout our lives, long before the moment of our own personal death arrives. Whenever someone close to us dies, some part of us dies with them. The experience of aging is itself a kind of dying, a letting go of our physical energy, perhaps even of our mental capacities. At any stage in life we can find ourselves dealing with very significant losses, such as the loss of a relationship, the loss of a job, the loss of our good name. In such losses, Easter, the feast of life, can speak powerfully to us. Because the Lord is risen, we do not face these losses alone. The risen Lord can work powerfully in all our experiences of loss and weakness.

All those to whom the risen Lord appears are sent out as messengers of Easter hope and joy, as agents of new life. Easter, the feast of life, sends all of us forth to create a culture of life. We are faithful to that Easter calling whenever we help others to make new beginnings, whenever we help those who are struggling to live life to the full, whenever we are present to people in ways that enable their gifts to come alive and be placed at the service of others. Easter reminds us of our calling to be agents of God's life-giving work in our world. This is our baptismal calling. Easter is a day to renew our response to our baptismal calling.

Second Sunday of Easter

Facing our doubts

Acts 4:32-5; 1 Jn 5:1-6; Jn 20:19-31

Sometimes people of faith can worry when they sense that doubts have crept into their faith. They sense that their faith is not as strong as it used to be because they have all these doubts that they never had in the past. Because of their doubts, prayer does not come as easy to them. They feel that they are no longer on the same wavelength as other people of faith. They start to compare their own faith unfavourably with the faith of others. Yet, faith and doubt are inseparable companions. Some of the Church's saints were plagued with doubt and suffered a great darkness of spirit. Saint Thérèse of Lisieux comes to mind in that regard. In more recent times, some of the writings of Mother Teresa of Calcutta have revealed that she went through a time of great spiritual darkness and doubt.

Thomas Merton was a Cistercian monk who wrote many books that have been an inspiration to many people. He died about twenty years ago. In his book *Asian Journal* he wrote, 'Faith is not the suppression of doubt. It is the overcoming of doubt and you overcome doubt by going through it. The person of faith who has never experienced doubt is not a person of faith.' We often have to pass through a period of great religious doubt and scepticism to pass over into a deeper certitude, a certitude which is not just a human certitude but the certitude of God within us.

The Gospels suggest that those closest to Jesus were no strangers to doubt. In today's Gospel reading from John, we meet the figure of Thomas. After the risen Lord appeared to the disciples, they went to Thomas with their wonderful news, the Easter Gospel, 'We have seen the Lord.' Thomas could not bring himself to share their Easter faith; he doubted that what they said could be true. He was like a wall, a block that stopped the good news cold. He laid down very clear conditions before he would believe. He insisted not only on seeing the risen Lord but on putting his finger into holes that the nails had made in Jesus' hands and feet and putting his hand into the wound in Jesus' side. Here was someone who wanted physical evidence before he would believe. He needed proof of a kind that would banish all doubt. It can be somewhat disconcerting for people of faith to come up against that kind of attitude. They feel helpless before it. When parents who are people of faith encounter such an attitude in their own children it can be especially distressing.

Yet, we cannot force our faith on those who are in a place of doubt, no more than others can force their faith on us when we are in that place. We need to accommodate ourselves to those who cannot share our faith, for whatever reason. This is what we find Jesus doing in the Gospel reading. When he appears again to the disciples, this time with Thomas present, he doesn't reprimand Thomas for his refusal to believe. He meets Thomas in the place where Thomas is, in that place of honest doubt, and he accommodates himself to the conditions that Thomas laid down, inviting him to touch the wounds of his crucifixion. He then gently invites Thomas to move on from doubt to faith, 'Doubt no longer but believe'. The risen Lord is constantly calling on all of us to go through our doubt and out beyond it into a rich and full Easter faith. He continues to call in that way, even when there is no response forthcoming.

The response of Thomas to that call of the risen Lord is very striking. Out of the mouth of the great doubter comes one of the greatest confessions of faith in the Gospels, 'My Lord and my God'. It is a confession of faith that has resonated with believers ever since. We often recite it together as one of the responses after the moment of consecration in the Mass. It is often the case that those who have plumbed the depths of great religious doubt and scepticism emerge from that experience as people of unshakable faith. It is as if their faith has been honed and purified in the cauldron of doubt.

Thomas joined the ranks of those who saw and believed. However, after Thomas' great profession of faith, Jesus goes on to pronounce a beatitude upon all those who believe without having seen the risen Lord in the way Thomas and the other disciples saw him. Jesus' beatitude embraces all future generations of believers, including all of us gathered here today. We might be inclined to think that those to whom the risen Lord appeared are more privileged than we are. Yet, Jesus' beatitude hints that a greater blessedness rests upon those who believe without having seen. The risen Lord is as present to us in as real a way as he was to those eyewitnesses, through the community of faith, through the Eucharist and through his word. Through all these channels of his presence, the risen Lord calls out to us, 'Doubt no longer but believe'.

Third Sunday of Easter

The Lord's faithful coming

Acts 3:13-15, 17-19; 1 Jn 2:1-5; Lk 24:35-48

Paul Verlaine was a nineteenth-century French poet. His early life was somewhat on the wild side. He was imprisoned for a time for having shot at his companion, a fellow poet. While he was in prison he had something of a conversion. His poems written while in prison are very moving. In one of his poems he addresses the risen Lord, 'Lord … Beneath this troubled canopy where my heart has been digging out its tomb and where I feel the heavens flow towards me I ask you, by what road you'd have me come.' He is asking the Lord to show him the road on which he could come to him. Later in the same poem, the Lord says to him, 'It is not you who must come to me; it is I who have chosen to come to you. Look at my hands stretched out to you. Here, eat; be nourished. Let your mind be opened to understand.' Verlaine came to understand that, rather than having to find the right road along which to come to the Lord, it was the Lord who was coming to him. He realised that the gap between himself and the Lord would be bridged by the Lord rather than by himself.

Verlaine's uncertain mood in prison must have been similar to how the disciples felt after Good Friday. They had broken their relationship with Jesus by abandoning him when he needed them most. They had created a gap between themselves and the Lord; they must have felt that this gap was unbridgeable. There was no road they could take to undo what had been done. Yet, on that first Easter Sunday they discovered that the gap they had created between themselves and the Lord was bridged by the Lord. They could not come to him, but he came to them. Today's Gospel reading suggests that when the Lord came to them, they found it almost impossible to believe. When he appeared among them, and said to them, 'Peace be with you', their reaction was one of alarm and fright. They were agitated and full of doubt. They thought he could not be real; they presumed they were seeing a ghost. How could someone whom they had betrayed, denied and abandoned be standing among them now, offering them the gift of his peace, the gift of his reconciling love?

We are in the season of Easter, which is seven weeks long. The Church gives us this lengthy period of Easter to help us reflect on the various dimensions of the meaning of Easter. Easter has many messages which are vitally important to us, the Lord's followers, today. One of the messages the feast of Easter proclaims is the Lord's faithfulness to us, in spite of our unfaithfulness to him. Because of our various failures and weaknesses, we can sometimes find ourselves wondering by what road we can come to the Lord from whom we have turned away. In response to that anxiety, the Lord says to us, 'It is not you who must come to me; it is I who have chosen to come to you.' We can find that good news hard to believe at times. As was the case with the disciples in today's Gospel reading, doubts can rise in our hearts. Having failed to love the Lord in various ways, we doubt that he could love us in this all-forgiving way. Yet, this is at the heart of the message of Easter. Easter invites us to open ourselves to the coming of the risen Lord who loves us in our weakness and frailty and empowers us to go forth renewed.

According to today's Gospel reading, the risen Lord broke through the self-doubt of his disciples in three ways. He firstly showed them his wounds. These weren't just any old wounds. They were the wounds of that greater love which led Jesus to lay down his life for all. He continues to show us his wounds today, to bring home to us the depth of his love for us and the extent of his faithfulness to us. The Lord then opened the scriptures for his disciples to help them to see that what happened to him, including his passion and death, was already contained within the Jewish scriptures. The risen Lord continues to speak to us today through the scriptures. He is present to us in his word, the word of the Lord. Finally, the risen Lord then shared a simple meal with his disciples to convince them that he wanted to be in communion with them even though they had failed him. The Lord continues to call us to his table today. It is above all at the table of the Eucharist that he enters into communion with us and invites us to enter into communion with him. It is in the Eucharist that we can really appreciate that the Lord has chosen to come to us in our brokenness and weakness. It is from the Eucharist that he sends us out in the power of his presence to be his witnesses in the world.

Fourth Sunday of Easter *Hearing the call of the Good Shepherd*

Acts 4:8–12; 1 Jn 3:1–2; Jn 10:11–18

When people go to Rome, one of the places they often visit is the catacombs, the earliest Christian cemeteries in existence. The earliest Christian art is to be found in the catacombs. The images are very simple and unadorned compared to the Christian art that would emerge in later centuries. Yet the art is very striking just because of its simplicity and its directness. One way in which Jesus is represented in this early Christian art is as the Good Shepard. An image in the catacomb of St Callistus depicts Jesus the Good Shepherd as a young beardless man with a sheep draped around his shoulders holding a bucket of water in his right hand. Clearly the image of Jesus as the Good Shepherd that we find in today's Gospel reading spoke to Christians from the earliest days of the Church.

Perhaps one of the reasons why the image appealed to Christians from the very earliest years of the Church is because it conveyed something of the personal nature of the relationship between Jesus and his followers. That image from the catacombs conveys a sense of the close personal connection that the shepherd has with the sheep. The shepherd has gone looking for the one sheep that has wandered off and having found it is taking the sheep home on his shoulders back to the flock. There is a connection between the shepherd and this one sheep. That is what Jesus conveys in today's Gospel reading. He declares that he knows his own and his own know him, just as the Father knows him and he knows the Father. It is an extraordinary statement to make. Jesus is saying that the very personal relationship that he has with his heavenly father is the model for the very personal relationship that he has with each one of us. Jesus knows us as intimately as the Father knows him, and he wants us to know him as intimately as he knows the Father. There is a great deal to ponder there. When it comes to the Lord we are not just one of a crowd, lost in a sea of faces. In a way that we will never fully understand, the Lord knows each one of us by name. He relates to us in a personal way and he invites us to relate to him in a personal way. He wishes to enter into a personal relationship with each one of us. I am often struck by a line in St Paul's letter to the churches in Galatia where he says, 'I live by faith in the Son of God who loved me and gave himself for me.' We can each make our own those words of St Paul. When Jesus says in today's Gospel reading that, as the Good Shepherd, 'I lay down my life for my sheep', he is saying that he lays down his life for each one of us individually.

The Lord who knows us by name, who gave himself in love for each one of us, also calls us by name. The Lord has a calling that is personal to each one of us. He calls us in our uniqueness with our very particular temperament, our unique identity, the background that is specific to each one of us. No one of us is like anyone else. Parents know how distinct and unique each of their children is. They will all have been given the same love; they grow up in basically the same environment. Yet, from a very early age, their uniqueness becomes very evident. The family is a microcosm of the Church as a whole. From the time of our Baptism, we are each called to be the Lord's disciples, to follow the Good Shepherd. However, the way we do that will be unique to each one of us. The particular way in which the Lord works through us is unique to each one of us. I can do something for the Lord that only I can do. Each person in this church can do something for the Lord that only he or she can do. Each one of us has a unique contribution to make to the work of the Lord in the world, to the life of the Church, and that contribution is just as important as anyone else's contribution. We each have a unique vocation and each vocation is equally significant. Each one of us is vitally important to the Lord. When we each respond to our unique vocation, we give a lift to everyone else. When any one of us fails to respond to that vocation, we are all a little bit impoverished.

The first reading declares that the stone that was rejected by the builders proved to be the keystone. There is a clear reference there to Jesus himself, the rejected one. We can all feel at times like the rejected stone, for whatever reason. Yet, we are never rejected in the Lord's eyes. He continues to call us in the way that is unique to us. He sees us as the keystone for some aspect of his work. He recognises the potential for good that is within us all. Today we are invited to commit ourselves anew to hearing and responding to the call of the Good Shepherd.

Fifth Sunday of Easter   *Our dependence on the Lord*

Acts 9:26–31; 1 Jn 3:18–24; Jn 15:1–8

We live in an age that tends to put a high value on independence. We like to feel that we have our destiny in our own hands. One of the aspects of reaching old age that can trouble us is the prospect of losing our independence. We want to be as independent as possible for as long as possible. Yet, we are also aware that independence is a relative thing. We know that we depend on each other in all kinds of ways all through life. We are totally dependent on others at the beginning of life, and probably for many of us, at the end of life as well. In between the beginning and end of life, we never escape fully from that dependency on others. In living our lives, there will always be a certain degree of tension between our need to assert our independence of others and our recognition that we are dependent on others.

The Gospel's perspective on that basic tension in human life tends to put more emphasis on our dependence than on our independence. In this respect, as in others, the Gospel message is at odds with the culture in which we live. The Gospel strongly proclaims our ultimate dependence on God, and also our dependence on each other, because one of the primary ways that God is present to us is through each other. The first Christians had a stronger sense than we do of their dependence on one another, if they were to become all that God was calling them to be. Saint Paul's vision of the Church as the body of Christ speaks of a community of believers who are mutually interdependent. As Paul says, 'the eye cannot say to the hand, "I have no need of you", nor again the head to the feet, "I have no need of you". Paul himself, the great missionary, was aware of his dependence on others in the Church. In today's first reading Luke describes a moment in Paul's early life as a Christian when he was very dependent on one person in particular, Barnabas. Paul had only recently changed from being one of the most zealous persecutors of the Church to being one of its most enthusiastic missionaries. He very much wanted to join the community of disciples in Jerusalem but, given his former reputation, they were all afraid of him and kept him at a distance. It took Barnabas to convince everyone that Paul was a changed person. Paul would go on to be a much more significant person in the early Church than Barnabas. Yet, he was completely dependent on Barnabas to create that initial opening for him. Paul was aware that his dependence on Barnabas, and on others in the course of his life, was an expression of his dependence on the Lord who came to him through others.

Jesus' image of the vine in the Gospel reading, like Paul's image of the body, suggests how we as believers are dependent on each other and, ultimately, on the Lord, if we are to live as the Lord's disciples. Jesus states, 'a branch cannot bear fruit all by itself'. We cannot live fruitful lives as Christians by going it alone. We need the community of believers if we are to become all that our Baptism calls us to be. We need to be connected in some way into the community of faith, what we call the Church. It is only in communion with other believers that our lives can bear the fruit of the Spirit. It is in and through other believers that the Lord can nurture our faith so that it shapes more and more of our lives. That community of believers that we need to be in communion with will often be a mixed bag. In another image that Jesus uses, it will be a mixture of wheat and weeds, as indeed each one of us is. Yet, it is there that we find the Lord in a privileged way and it is through our connection with the Church that we are connected to him. That connection with the Lord is vital if we are to live our Baptism to the full; it is on him that we are ultimately dependent. We need the Lord if our lives are to bear the fruit of the Spirit. As Jesus states in the Gospel reading, 'Cut off from me you can do nothing.'

If we are dependent on the Lord, there is a sense in which he is also dependent on us. In the Gospel reading Jesus says, 'Whoever remains in me … bears fruit in plenty.' We would all consider fruit to be healthy food; it is an important source of nourishment. Lives that bear fruit in plenty are lives that nurture others, that are life-giving for others. The Lord depends on us to feed each other with his love and his presence. He needs us to give concrete expression to his love for others. We can only do this if we are connected to the vine, if we are in union with the Lord and his disciples.

Sixth Sunday of Easter *Choosing the one who has chosen us*

Acts 10:25-26, 34-35, 44-48; 1 Jn 4:7-10; Jn 15:9-17

We all make choices in the course of our lives, some of which are more fundamental than others. There are simple choices we make every day as we go about our lives that do not fundamentally influence who we are or how we live. Then there are the more significant choices that shape us for life. We chose someone as a friend and if the choice is mutual it can have a powerful influence for good on the rest of our lives. A man and a woman chose each other as husband and wife and their lives are profoundly transformed as a result of that mutual choice. Those really significant choices in life are not made in an instant. We have to grow into such choices. We build up to making them and, once made, we must work at being faithful to them. They are not so much choices that we make as choices that we live.

In today's Gospel reading, Jesus declares to his disciples, 'You did not choose me, no I chose you.' Jesus was saying to his disciples and to us that his choice of them, his choice of us, came first. The Lord has chosen each one of us, in love. He has chosen to befriend us, as Jesus says in that Gospel reading, 'I call you friends.' We don't have to go looking for the Lord's friendship; it is a given. Some of us may have had the experience of looking for someone's friendship but not finding it. We would like to befriend someone, but he or she doesn't seem as keen to befriend us. It is a friendship we seek but always eludes us. We will also have had the experience of someone simply choosing us as a friend. They offer us the gift of friendship unconditionally; we don't have to go searching for it. It is a given. The only issue is whether we wish to reciprocate and choose the one who has chosen us. That second situation corresponds to how the Lord relates to us, 'I call you friends ... I have chosen you', he says.

The Lord's choice of us is not in doubt. The only issue is whether we choose him who has chosen us. This is what Jesus calls for in today's Gospel reading. Having said to his disciples, 'As the Father has loved me, so I have loved you,' he immediately says, 'Remain in my love.' This is the first thing we have to do. As one writer that I came across recently put it, 'It is not just to live in a religion, but to live in the love with which Jesus loves us, the love that he has received from the Father.' That is the core of everything, to remain in the Lord's love as he remains in the Father's love. Throughout the centuries disciples of Jesus have encountered uncertainties, conflicts and difficulties of every kind. Yet, in the midst of it all, the important thing is to remain in that relationship of love that the Lord has initiated with us.

To remain in the love of Jesus is not something theoretical. Jesus tells us what it entails in that Gospel reading. It means to 'keep my commandments' which he immediately sums up in one commandment, 'This is my commandment. Love one another as I have loved you.' Christians will find in their religion many commandments. Over time they increase in number. Only about the commandment to love does Jesus say, 'this is my commandment'. It is as if Jesus is saying, this is what all the commandments boil down to. As we remain in the love of Jesus for us, we allow that love to take hold of us and to flow through us to embrace others. A little earlier in John's Gospel Jesus refers to this commandment as 'new'. It is new with reference to all the other commandments that are in the Jewish scriptures. Its newness consists in that little word 'as'. We are to love one another as Jesus has loved us, as the Father has loved Jesus. This is a love which has no trace of self-interest or possessiveness or manipulation. It is the love that Jesus showed on the cross. It seems an extraordinary command; we are tempted to think it is beyond us. Yet, Jesus does not ask us to do the impossible. Before he asks us to do anything, he first calls on us to remain in his love, to receive his love into our hearts. Only then can we begin to love one another as he has loved us. Jesus does not give us this commandment as a law to regulate our lives, but as a source of joy. He declares in the Gospel reading, 'I have told you this so that my own joy may be in you and your joy be complete.' Without love it is not possible to move towards a more joyful, simple and delightful Christian faith. To the extent that love is at the heart of our faith, it will be a joyful faith, a sharing in the Lord's own joy.

The Ascension of the Lord   *The promise of leave-taking*

Acts 1:1–11; Eph 4:1–13; Mk 16:15–20

We have all had the experience of leaving some place that has been very significant for us and moving on to another place. At a certain age, young people feel the need to leave home, a place that has been hugely significant for them, where they have received love and have been nurtured in various ways. Leaving home is often a difficult experience emotionally for young people and yet, it also holds the promise of something new. Many of us will have had the experience of having to let go of those who have been dear to us and who move on from us. In the case of young people moving on from home, it can be more difficult for the parents than for the young person involved. Yet, painful as it is for parents, they too can have a sense that there is something promising about their son or daughter moving on and leaving home. It is a pattern that is deeply rooted in life; those we love invariably move on from us in some way. The pain of moving on for both those doing the moving on and those who struggle to let go can ultimately be very life-giving for everyone involved. The leave-taking can open up a whole new horizon which can be full of promise for all. A young person leaves home, falls in love, gets married and returns to the home of their parents on a regular basis with children in tow. The beginning of a new life for the young person, which leaving made possible, can be the beginning of a new life for parents as well. The experience of loss, with all its heartbreak, can give way to an experience of receiving something new and wonderful that would not have been possible without the initial loss. Our faith teaches us that this is true of even the most traumatic experience of loss, the loss involved in death. We are letting go of our loved one to a new and fuller life, which we hope one day to share with them.

We celebrate today the feast of the Ascension of the Lord. The Lord's ascension marked the end of that period during which the risen Lord was visibly present to his disciples. This entailed an experience of loss for the first disciples. It was not as painful as the loss they had experienced when Jesus was crucified. On the third day after the crucifixion, the risen Lord appeared to them. He spoke to his disciples, as he had spoken to them before his death; he ate with them, as he had eaten with them before his death. Their sorrow gave way to joy, their despair to hope, their fear to courage. Yet, even this wonderful period during which they saw the risen Lord had to come to an end. They had to learn to let Jesus go again. The struggle to do that is captured in today's first reading. As the risen Lord takes his leave of them, they were staring into the sky. It calls to mind the experience of people at an airport seeing off their loved ones. They keep their loved ones in view until it becomes impossible to see them any longer. Yet, the disciples' experience of loss at the time of the ascension of the Lord was very different in quality to their experience of loss at the time of his crucifixion. Jesus was no longer dead; he was alive with a new life, and he promised that he would come back to them in and through the Holy Spirit. In today's first reading he tells them, 'You will receive power when the Holy Spirit comes on you.' The Lord would be with them in and through the Holy Spirit. Yes, he was leaving them, but it was a leaving that would make possible a new presence. Today's Gospel reading says that after the Lord was taken up from his disciples into heaven, the same Lord was working with the disciples as they proclaimed the Gospel.

That is the real meaning of the feast of the Ascension. We celebrate today the many ways that the Lord works with us. It is not so much a feast of the Lord's departure but a feast of his active and life-giving presence among us. As people of faith, we can get discouraged by the decline in faith today, which finds expression in so many ways. Yet, today's feast reminds us that the Lord never stops working among us. When it comes to the work that flows from faith, we may get tired and discouraged, but the Lord never tires. As St Paul reminds us in today's second reading, the risen Lord has given us a share in his own grace. He keeps on bestowing his gifts upon us, different gifts to different people, so that as individuals and as a church, we can become fully mature with his own fullness. Today's feast calls on us to keep on receiving from the Lord who is always giving to us and is always working among us so that his vision for human living continues to be proclaimed.

Pentecost Sunday
The signs of the Holy Spirit

Acts 2:1–11; Gal 5:16–25; Jn 15:26–7; 16:12–15

When you look around our parish church, there is no shortage of images: statues, paintings, stained glass, carvings and plaster moulds. They are mostly images of Jesus, Mary and of the saints. The Holy Spirit, whose feast we celebrate today, does not easily lend itself to imagery. One traditional image of the Holy Spirit is the dove. That is drawn from the Gospel accounts of the Baptism of Jesus. However, the language of the evangelists in that passage is very tentative. They simply say that the Holy Spirit descended on Jesus like a dove, in the way that a dove might descend. There are two other images of the Holy Spirit in today's first reading. There again the language is suggestive rather than descriptive. Luke says that all who gathered in one room heard what sounded like a powerful wind from heaven and that something appeared to them that seemed like tongues of fire. The evangelists do not say that there was an actual dove at the Baptism of Jesus, or that there was an actual wind and fire at Pentecost. There is something about the Holy Spirit that does not lend itself to any kind of concrete representation, because the Holy Spirit cannot be seen. Yet, the Holy Spirit is profoundly real.

There is a great deal in our universe that is real but is not visible to the naked eye. We may need a microscope or a powerful telescope to see it. What we see with our eyes is only a fraction of our physical world. The Holy Spirit is part of the spiritual world, and so is beyond the range of scientific instruments. Yet, there are helpful ways of imagining the Holy Spirit. In today's second reading, St Paul, uses an image drawn from nature; he refers to the fruit of the Spirit, which is the visible expression of the Spirit in someone's life. We may not be able to see the Holy Spirit, but we can see the impact of the Spirit in a human life, just as we cannot see the wind but we can see the impact of the wind on people and objects. Paul is saying, 'Wherever you find love, joy, peace, patience, kindness, goodness, trustfulness, gentleness and self-control, the Spirit is at work.' The Spirit becomes visible in and through these qualities, these virtues. The person who possessed those qualities in abundance was Jesus because he was full of the Holy Spirit, full of the life of God. The Holy Spirit is essentially the life of God, and God's life is a life of love. It is that divine life, that divine love, which was poured out at Pentecost, initially on the first disciples and then on all believers, including ourselves today. Saint Paul expresses it very simply in his letter to the Romans, 'God's love has been poured into our hearts through the Holy Spirit that has been given to us.' That Spirit of God's love works within us to bear the rich fruit that Paul speaks about in today's second reading. The ordinary, day-to-day expressions of goodness and kindness, of faithfulness and self-control, of patience and gentleness, are all manifestations of the Spirit that has been given to us by God. The spiritual, in that sense, is not something otherworldly; it is humanity at its best.

We have an example of humanity at its best in today's first reading. On that first Pentecost, there was a wonderful communion between people from all over the Roman Empire. They were united in hearing in their own native language the preaching of the first disciples about the marvels of God. In spite of differences of language and culture, there was a profound communion among them. Wherever we find such communion of heart and spirit today among those who are strikingly different, there the Holy Spirit is at work. Unity in diversity is the mark of the Spirit, the fruit of the Spirit. In the Gospel reading Jesus points out another role of the Spirit in our lives, and that is the pursuit of truth. Jesus declares that one of the Spirit's roles is to lead us to the complete truth. Whenever someone has a genuine openness to truth, a willingness to search for truth even when it challenges our convictions, there the Spirit is at work. Full truth is always beyond us;

we never possess it completely. In John's Gospel Jesus declares himself to be the truth and he is always beyond us; we never fully possess him in this life. One of the roles of the Spirit is to lead us towards Jesus who is the complete truth, and to give us the courage to bear witness to his truth. In the Gospel reading Jesus says, 'The Spirit of Truth shall be my witness', and then he immediately says 'and you will be witnesses.' It is the Spirit who gives us the courage to witness Jesus the Truth, his teaching, his way of life, his values and attitudes. We need the courage that the Spirit of Truth gives us today more than ever.

ORDINARY
TIME

The Most Holy Trinity

God as a community of love

Deut 4:32-4, 39-40; Rm 8:14-17; Mt 28:16-20

It is probably true to say that most of us know only a few people really well. A husband and wife may know more or less all that there is to know about each other. The same could be said of two people who have been very close friends for many years. Yet, even those who spend a lot of time in each other's company don't always know each other fully. Family members and friends can continue to surprise us. We are complex beings, all of us. Not only are we complex but most of us do not find it easy to reveal ourselves to someone. It is not surprising that we struggle to understand each other.

If we struggle to grasp each other, we might wonder what chance we have of understanding God. God is infinitely more mysterious than any human being. The earliest theologian of the Church, St Paul, writes in letter to the Romans, 'O the depth of the riches and wisdom and knowledge of God! How unsearchable are his judgements and how inscrutable his ways!' Paul was acknowledging there that God is, in a sense, beyond us. When it comes to speaking about God, human language is totally inadequate. Yet, we must talk about God, while acknowledging that our talking about God never does justice to God. There is more to God that we can ever hope to put into words and, yet, words are all we have.

Today's feast is the feast of the Most Holy Trinity. Those words, 'Most Holy Trinity' are an effort to express an important truth about who God is. As Christians we believe that, although God is mysterious, Jesus is the fullest revelation of God possible in human form. It is Jesus who reveals God to be Trinity. If Jesus had not lived we would never come to think of God in this way. Those who do not recognise Jesus as the fullest revelation of God possible in human form do not believe that God is Trinity.

The Jews had a very strong conviction about the oneness of God; there is one God and no other. We find that stated very clearly in today's first reading: 'The Lord is God indeed, he and no other.' The first Christians, who were Jews, shared that conviction. However, because of all that Jesus said and did, they recognised that within this oneness of God, there was a wonderful diversity. They came to understand that if God is one, he is one community. Jesus' life, death and Resurrection revealed to them that within God there is a communion of love between the Father, the Son and the Holy Spirit. The life of God is a relational life where love is given and received in the fullest possible way. The Church eventually came to express this insight that God is community by speaking of God as a trinity of persons who are perfectly one while remaining distinct.

This is a very rich understanding of God and it is one that distinguishes Christianity from all other world religions. It has important implications for what human life is about and what we as a church are about. If we are made in the image and likeness of God and the one God is a community of persons, then our calling is to live in community, to give and to receive love. We are most God-like when we are in communion with others, when we love others as God the Father loves Jesus and as Jesus has loved us, when our love for each other is the fruit of the Holy Spirit. Such loving relationships are a wonderful blessing; we are at our best when we are in them; they bring the best out in us.

Our calling is not only to build communities that reflect the community that is God. There is another dimension to our calling which is even more fundamental. We are called into the communal life that is God. God wants to draw us into God's own life. At the very beginning of our Christian life, as Jesus reminds us in the Gospel reading, we are baptised in the name of the Father, Son and Holy Spirit; we are baptised into the life of the Trinity. Saint Paul spells that out in today's second reading. Through Baptism we receive the Holy Spirit who makes us cry out with Jesus, 'Abba, Father'. Through the Holy Spirit, God the Father unites us to his son, inspiring us to cry out 'Abba, Father', as Jesus does. It is extraordinary to think that we are invited to have the same relationship with God the Father that Jesus has and that the Holy Spirit makes this possible. We are called into a very intimate relationship with God, Father, Son and Spirit.

It is in allowing ourselves to be drawn into the communal life of God in this way that we in turn are enabled to form communities that reflect the life of God. In that sense, there is a twofold movement in our lives as Christians which continues throughout our lives. We are continually drawn into the life of God and sent forth to form relationships that give expression to the relational life of God.

The Body and Blood of Christ   *A celebration of communion*

Ex 24:3-8; Heb 9:11-15; Mk 14:12-16, 22-6

The feast of the Body and Blood of Christ, the feast of Corpus Christi, celebrates the centrality of the Eucharist in the life of the Church. The central place of the Eucharist in the life of the Church goes back ultimately to that short story that we read from Mark's Gospel in our Gospel reading today. It is the account of what Jesus said and did at the last supper.

We notice just how carefully Jesus prepared for that meal. He sent two of his disciples into Jerusalem to meet up with a designated person who would know the room where Jesus could celebrate the Passover meal with his disciples. It seems as if everything was well prepared in advance. The attention to detail suggests the huge importance of this meal to Jesus. After Jesus' death and Resurrection, this meal was remembered as having a great significance. That was because at that final meal Jesus did something he had never done at any of his previous meals with his disciples. He took the bread and the wine that were two of the staple ingredients of every Jewish meal, including the solemn Passover meal, and he blessed the bread, broke it, gave it to his disciples saying, 'This is my body', and then blessed the cup of wine, and gave it to his disciples saying, 'This is my blood, the blood of the covenant, which is to be poured out for many.' There were momentous actions and words. Jesus was giving himself to his disciples under the form of bread and wine, and through them, to all humanity. He was anticipating the gift of himself he would make the following day, on Calvary.

As well as symbolically anticipating what would happen the following day, what Jesus said and did at that last supper was the culmination of his whole ministry, his pouring out of himself in love for others during the previous three years. That meal brought together in one moment all he had done as well as all he had yet to do; it looked back to the relatively recent past and to the imminent future. Because that meal was a Jewish Passover meal, it also looked back to the distant past, to the first Passover, just before God led his people out of the slavery of Egypt. Jesus was now about to lead God's people out of the slavery of sin. It also looked forward to the distant future, to the kingdom of God in heaven. At that meal, according to Mark, Jesus said, 'I shall not drink any more wine until the day I drink the new wine in the kingdom of God.' The last supper looked forward to the future heavenly banquet, at which people from north, south, east and west would gather.

This was a hugely significant meal when the past and the future, time and eternity, all came together, when Jesus expressed in very simple gestures and words the essence of his identity and his mission. From the very earliest days the community of disciples gathered to repeat what Jesus said and did at the last supper, in response to his command, 'Do this in memory of me'. In saying 'Do this in memory of me' Jesus was showing that he wanted this last supper to be, not just the last in a series of meals, but the beginning of a new series of meals. As a result, the last supper was also the first Eucharist. As Jesus gave himself to his disciples at the last supper, the risen Lord would continue to give himself to his disciples at every Eucharist. As Jesus entered into a very personal communion with his disciples at the last supper, he would enter into an equally personal communion with all future disciples at every Eucharist. Saint Paul said to the Church in Corinth, 'the cup of blessing that we bless, is it not a communion in the blood of Christ? The bread that we break, is it not a communion in the body of Christ?' Jesus wants to enter into communion with us in the Eucharist. In saying to his disciples at the last supper and to each of us today, 'Take and eat. Take and drink', he is calling on us to enter into communion with him.

At the Eucharist, we state that we want to be in communion with the Lord and with all that he professes and values. We also state that we want to be in communion with each other, because there can be no communion with the Lord without communion with one another, and with all of creation. As Paul again said to the Church of Corinth, 'Because there is one bread, we who are many are one body, for we all partake of the one bread.' At every Eucharist, we are making a very significant statement about who we are, who we want to be and how we want to live. Every Eucharist is a renewal of our baptismal identity. At every Eucharist, just as Jesus says to us, 'Take, this is my body ... this is my blood', we say to him, 'Take, this is my body; this is my blood. Here I am. I give myself to you and to all those whom you love, just as you give yourself to me and to all who come to you.'

Second Sunday in Ordinary Time

Opening a door for the Lord

1 Sm 3:3-10, 19; 1 Cor 6:13-15, 17-20; Jn 1:35-42

We can probably all think of people who opened doors for us in life. Perhaps at a crucial moment in our lives they pointed us in the right direction. They were an influence for good on us; maybe they shared with us some gift they possessed, or allowed us to benefit from an experience they had or some discovery they made. We appreciate these people because they had the freedom and the generosity to give something worthwhile away for the benefit of others, rather than keeping it to themselves.

That is how John the Baptist is portrayed in the Gospel reading this Sunday. He had come to recognise Jesus as a very special revelation of God's love. Far from keeping that discovery to himself, he shared it with his own disciples, even though he knew that in doing so he was going to lose them to Jesus. He pointed two of his disciples in the direction of Jesus. He opened a door for them, even though it would mean a loss for himself. A short while later, one of those two disciples, Andrew, did for his brother Simon what John the Baptist had done for him. He led his brother to Jesus. In the first reading, Eli did something similar for Samuel, helping him to hear God's call. The readings this Sunday put before us three people, Eli, John the Baptist and Andrew, each of whom in different ways pointed others in the right direction, led others to the one who is the source of life.

We could probably all identify a John the Baptist or an Andrew or an Eli in our own lives, people who, in some way or another, brought us to the Lord, or helped us to recognise and receive the Lord who was present to us. We might think first of our own parents who brought us to the baptismal font as infants. As early as possible into our lives they wanted to say to us what John the Baptist said to his disciples, 'Look, there is the lamb of God.' Then, in the following years, they may have helped us to grow in our relationship with the Lord into whom we had been baptised, bringing us to the church, praying with us, reading stories from the Gospels to us, taking us to see the crib at Christmas, placing an image of the Lord or of one of the saints in our room, helping us to prepare for the sacraments of the Eucharist and Confirmation. If we were fortunate, we might have had a good religion teacher at school who took us a step further in our relationship with the Lord, who enabled us to 'come and see', in the words of the Gospel reading today. I went to secondary school with the De La Salle brothers and one of them brought us through the Gospel of Luke in religion class. Looking back, he was sharing with us his own relationship with the Lord. It made a deep impression on me at the time.

Samuel who was led to the Lord by Eli is described in the first reading as a boy. In the Gospel reading, the two disciples who were led to the Lord by John the Baptist, and Simon who was led there by Andrew, were all adults. It was as adults that they allowed themselves to be directed towards the person of Jesus. In our adult years, we too may have met people who helped us to grow in our relationship with the Lord. There can come a time in our adult life, when we are very open to a reawakening, a deepening, of our faith. We may find ourselves searching for something more than we presently experience. The first words of Jesus to the disciples of John the Baptist took the form of the question, 'What do you want?' or 'What are you searching for?' Jesus sought to engage with those who were searching. He enters our adult lives in response to our deepest longings. In our searching, we can meet someone or some group who opens a door for us into a deeper relationship with the Lord. Through them the Lord can reach us and touch our lives in a way he had never done before.

At any time in our adult life we can meet a John the Baptist who says to us, 'Look, there is the Lamb of God', and that can happen to us over and over again, right up to the very end of our lives. The Lord never ceases to call us through others into a deeper relationship with himself. Indeed, there can come a time when the Lord asks any one of us to be a John the Baptist or an Andrew or an Eli for somebody else. He may call us to share our faith in some simple way, to open a door to the Lord for others. Our response to such a call can take many different forms. For Eli it took the form of helping the younger Samuel to find the right words for his prayer. For Andrew, it took the form of sharing a significant experience with his brother. The readings this Sunday invite us to be open to the many ways the Lord can draw us to himself, and also to the ways that he may be calling us to help him in drawing others to himself.

Third Sunday in Ordinary Time   *Someone worth following*

Jon 3:1-5, 10; 1 Cor 7:29-31; Mk 1:14-20

I had the good fortune to visit the Holy Land twice in recent years. On both occasions, one of the highlights was the boat trip onto the Sea of Galilee. A boat took the group out from the shore and after some time the engines were turned off and there in the silence on this wonderful inland lake we prayed. In the silence, it wasn't difficult to imagine Jesus engaged in his ministry by the shores of this sea. I was reminded of this experience by today's Gospel reading, Mark's account of Jesus' call of his first disciples. Jesus was the son of a carpenter, but his first followers were fishermen. It seems that they were very successful fishermen too. According to the Gospel reading, the father of James and John had a sufficiently large and successful fishing business to be able to give employment to several people. Peter, Andrew, James and John may not have been rich but they were not desperately poor. They obviously earned a good living from catching the fish that thrived in the fertile Sea of Galilee. When Jesus called these four men to follow him, they had something to leave behind. They turned their back on a successful business to give themselves over to staying in the company of Jesus, learning from all he said and did, and eventually being sent out by him as fishers of people, gathering them into God's kingdom.

We have an ecumenical Bible study group in Clontarf in the parish. It meets for a four or five week session a couple of times a year. The sharing that follows the input at these gatherings is always very rich. I was struck by the way that the faith sharing of those who were not Catholics was so obviously shaped by the hymns which they had been used to singing in church. I shared that impression at one of the meetings. One of the people who regularly attends these gatherings is a Methodist who plays the organ in a Church of Ireland parish. He sent me in the post a copy of some of the hymns that clearly meant a great deal to him. Today's Gospel reading brought to my mind one of those hymns. It is a hymn by a John G. Whittier, who lived from 1807 to 1892. One of the verses goes as follows, 'In simple trust like theirs who heard, beside the Syrian sea, the gracious calling of the Lord, let us like them, without a word, rise up and follow thee.' I was struck by that sentence: 'Let us like them, without a word, rise up and follow thee.' It brings home that the Gospel reading is not just about a group of fishermen two thousand years ago. It is very much about each one of us here today. Like them, we too have received the gracious calling of the Lord; like them, we too, without a word, are to rise up and follow Jesus in response to that calling.

Today's Gospel reading is a text around which we can all gather, regardless of our denominational backgrounds, because it brings us all back to basics. All of us who have been baptised into Christ are striving to follow him in response to his daily call. The more closely we follow the Lord, the closer we will come to each other. Very often, it is by our gathering around the word of the Lord, passages like today's Gospel reading, that we discover how close we are to each other in reality. Presumably, the reason that those first disciples left a thriving business to follow Jesus was because they had earlier experienced his message of good news. The core of that message of good news is to be found at the beginning of today's Gospel reading, 'The time has come and the kingdom of God is close at hand. Repent and believe the good news.' Jesus was announcing that God was powerfully at work in his words and in his deeds. People, like the fishermen, recognised God powerfully at work in all Jesus said and did. That is why they left everything to follow him.

That is why we follow Jesus today. As baptised Christians, we all recognise that God was powerfully at work in this unique human being and remains powerfully at work in him today as risen Lord. From within our different traditions, we have experienced the Lord as good news and, so, we want to answer his call. In answering that daily call we also recognise that we need to 'repent and believe' in the words of the Gospel reading. We need to keep on turning away from all that is not in keeping with the values of God's kingdom that Jesus proclaims. Yet, that turning away is always in the service of a turning towards, a turning towards the one who said of himself, 'I am the way, the truth and the life.' Turning towards the Lord will always entail turning towards others in mission. Part of our mission is helping others, especially our young people, to discover Jesus as someone who is still good news for us today, someone who is worth following because he is the way, the truth and the life.

Fourth Sunday in Ordinary Time   *Amazed at the Lord*

Deut 18:15–20; 1 Cor 7:32–5; Mk 1:21–8

We all have the capacity to stand amazed and astonished before something good and wonderful. By chance I tuned into a programme on the TV some time again about the first American astronauts to be sent into space in the early 1960s. This was long before any serious thought was given to putting a man on the moon. Several of them were being interviewed about the dangerous mission they had undertaken more than fifty years ago. More than one of them commented on the view of the earth from outer space. They were amazed and astounded at the extraordinary sight. It was the same for those astronauts many years later who looked back at the globe that was the earth from their position on the moon. They were awestruck by what they saw. Only a tiny percentage of humans will ever have such experiences. Yet, in other ways, I am sure, many of us will have found ourselves amazed and astonished before something or someone. The sight of a newborn child can inspire amazement and astonishment, especially when those looking on are the parents of the child.

The Gospel reading today refers to the people of Capernaum being astonished by Jesus' teaching and then by his subsequent action in releasing a man from his demons and restoring him to the community. In their astonishment, they started asking what it all meant. 'What is this?' they asked. Mark in his Gospel indicates that this was one of the ways people reacted to Jesus, with initial amazement, which lead to asking what it all meant. When Jesus and his disciples were caught in a storm at sea and Jesus calmed the storm with his authoritative word, Mark tells us that the disciples 'were filled with great awe, and said to one another, "Who then is this, that even the wind and the sea obey him?"' Whereas the people in Capernaum asked, 'What is this?' the disciples asked, 'Who is this?' The Lord's engagement with people left them amazed and astonished to the point that they wanted to know more about him and to understand who he was and what he was about.

Today's Gospel reading might prompt us to ask, 'To what extent am I amazed and astonished by the Lord and his Gospel?' It could be argued that our relationship with the Lord and his relationship with us is less immediate than was the case for the people of Capernaum or the disciples who travelled with him. Yet, the Jesus who was present to them is the same risen Lord who is present to all of us. The Lord's involvement with us has the potential to leave us astonished and asking the question 'Who is this?' We can, of course, lose that sense of excitement about our faith. Our relationship with the Lord, like all relationships, can become routine. The wonder and beauty of it all can cease to make any impression on us. We can take our faith for granted somewhat. It is worth holding on to that sense of amazement and excitement about our relationship with the Lord and his relationship with us, or trying to regain it if we have lost it. The Lord's teaching which so excited the people of Capernaum in the Gospel reading, retains the capacity to leave us amazed today. For that to happen we may need to hear it with new ears, to listen to it more attentively. That is the call which the responsorial psalm of today's Mass puts before us, 'O that today you would listen to his voice. Harden not your hearts'. We may need to sit with the Lord's word a little more, and allow it to speak to us and to reveal its richness. Then we can begin to discover that, yes, there is more here than we realised, there is richer fare here than we appreciated. Like the people in the Gospel story, we may find ourselves asking, 'What is this? Who is this?'

The people of Capernaum were amazed at Jesus' teaching; they were also amazed at his work in liberating the man in the synagogue from the demons that were tormenting and diminishing him. The Lord continues to work powerfully among us today. He works in life-giving ways in and through his followers, the members of his body, in and through all of us. In various ways, his liberating and life-giving work goes on in and through those who are open to being led by his Spirit. Despite the awful things that are happening in our world, goodness is all around us, and the Lord is powerfully active in the goodness of others. Here again we may need to step back, to pause and allow ourselves to be amazed and astonished by the goodness of others that we can sometimes take for granted, and to ask, 'What is this? Who is at work here?' There were many who saw what Jesus did and heard what he said and who were not amazed by it all. Many found what he said and did disturbing and wanted rid of him. We need a certain disposition of heart to be open to the wonder and beauty of the Lord's words and actions among us. We might pray for that disposition of heart today.

Fifth Sunday in Ordinary Time   *The dark side of faith*

Job 7:1-4, 6-7; 1 Cor 9:16-19, 22-3; Mk 1:29-39

We are all familiar with suffering in one shape or form, whether it is physical, emotional, mental or spiritual suffering. There is no getting away from suffering; it comes to us all and it comes in different guises at different times of our lives. To live is to suffer. Regardless of our differences, suffering is something we all have in common. Some people seem to suffer more than others. Yet, it is difficult to measure suffering, especially in others. There are some who do not seem to be suffering but are in great pain and others who seem to be suffering greatly but have a deep sense of peace.

The cry of Job in today's first reading is one that comes out of deep suffering. He is in a very dark place indeed. Not only has he lost his health, his property and members of his family but he seems to have lost God. He had been living an exemplary life and he cannot understand why God has allowed so much misfortune to befall him. The God whom he worshipped when times were good now seems a stranger to him. The God to whom he related as a friend now seems to have become his enemy. The experience of loss, whether it is the loss of health or property or loved ones, can bring on something of a spiritual crisis. Some can be tempted to abandon God, when their prayers out of the depths are not heard. They feel angry at God; they sense that their trust in God has not been vindicated. That is very much the place where Job finds himself in today's first reading. Job in that sense is every man or woman. The literary figure of Job is a very authentic depiction of the dark side of human experience, indeed, the dark side of faith in God.

The English writer C.S. Lewis was both a great intellectual and a man of deep faith. He set out to give a rational explanation for the Christian vision of life. In 1940 he wrote a book called *The Problem of Pain* in which he brought his intellect and his faith to bear on the problem of suffering. However, twenty-one years later, in 1961, he wrote a very different book, called *A Grief Observed*. In that book, he recognises that his rational, cerebral faith has taken something of a battering. The book consists of the painful and brutally honest reflections of a man whose wife died, slowly and in pain, from cancer. The book gives a vivid description of his own reaction, as a man of faith, to his wife's death. His rational faith fell to pieces when confronted with suffering of a devastatingly personal kind. He writes at one point, 'Where is God? Go to him when your need is desperate, when all other help is vain, and what do you find? A door slammed in your face and a sound of bolting and double bolting on the inside. After that, silence.' The name of Lewis's wife was Joy. He had earlier written a book called *Surprised by Joy* in which he wrote about the impact that his meeting her had on his life. His book *A Grief Observed* has received a wide readership because of his authentic and moving account of the impact of bereavement. Even though his faith was shaken because of Joy's death, Lewis did not lose it. Through the darkness of this experience he claims to have come to love his wife more truly. He writes that God had helped him to see that because the love he and his wife had for each other had reached its earthly limit, it was ready for its heavenly fulfilment.

Faith must come to terms with the cross and it is at the foot of the cross that faith can be purified and deepened. Jesus himself entered fully into the darkness of human suffering. In today's second reading, Paul says of himself, 'For the weak, I made myself weak.' That is certainly true of Jesus. He entered fully into the weakness of the human condition. Elsewhere, in one of his letters, Paul says of Christ that 'though he was rich, yet for your sakes he became poor, so that by his poverty you might become rich'. On the cross Jesus was at his weakest and poorest; it was on Calvary that, in the words of Lewis,

Jesus went to God and found a door slammed in his face, as he cried out, 'My God, my God, why have you forsaken me?' Yet, that cry of desolation is itself an act of faith; it is the language faith uses when confronted with the harrowing darkness of loss. God did not forsake Jesus, but brought him through death into the fullness of life. The Jesus who was crucified in weakness is the same risen Lord who is with us in our own experiences of suffering and desolation, just as he was with the suffering and the broken in today's Gospel reading. He is with us as one who knows our experience from the inside. Having gone down into the depths and having moved beyond the depths into a fuller life, he can enable us to do the same. He is the good shepherd who, even when we walk through the valley of darkness, is there with his crook and his staff, leading us to springs of living water.

Sixth Sunday in Ordinary Time   *Breaking out of isolation*

Lev 13:1-2, 44-6; 1 Cor 10:31-11:1; Mk 1:40-5

We all feel a need to connect with others, to be in communion with others. We don't like to feel isolated or cut off from family, friends, or the wider community. One of the most challenging aspects of sickness or physical disability can be the isolation that it brings. When we are ill or our body grows weak we cannot take the same initiative we used to take to connect with others. People can become housebound because of their physical condition; the things they used to do to meet up with others are no longer possible. Certain forms of illness can be more isolating than others. The most isolating form of illness in the time of Jesus was leprosy. For hygienic reasons, lepers had to live apart, 'outside the camp', in the words of today's first reading. Lepers were only allowed to have each other for company. They lived apart from their family, their friends and the community to which they belonged.

The leper in today's Gospel reading seemed determined to break out of his isolation. He did something that was unconventional and daring in approaching Jesus and pleading with him, 'If you want to, you can cure me.' His desperation to be healed of an illness that kept him totally isolated drove him to do something that was against the Jewish law at the time. In response to the leper's daring approach, Jesus did something just as unconventional. He reached out his hand and touched the leper. If it was forbidden for a leper to approach the healthy, it was certainly forbidden for a healthy person to touch a leper. It seems that the leper's desire to be freed from his isolation was met by an equally strong desire on the part of Jesus to deliver him from it. The Gospels portray Jesus as someone who worked to deliver people from their isolation, whether it is an isolation imposed by illness, as in the case of the leper, or by their lifestyle, as in the case of someone like Zacchaeus.

Both the person of Jesus and of the leper have something to say to us about steps we can take to connect with people, to break out of our isolation, even when the odds seem to be stacked against us. We can all be tempted from time to time to retreat into our shell, whether it is because of our health or some disability or some past experience that has drained us of life. It is at such times that we need something of the initiative and daring energy of the leper. There can come a time when, like the leper, we need to take our courage in our own hands and, against the conventional expectation, head out in some bold direction. It was desperation that drove the leper to seek out Jesus. Sometimes for us too, it can be our desperation that finally gets us going, gets us to connect with that person who matters to us and to whom we matter more than we realise or gets us to link up with some gathering or some group that has the potential to do us good or maybe even to transform our lives. Sometimes I can be amazed at the initiatives that some people take to connect with others, people who are much less healthy and much less physically able than I am. I am thinking of older people who have mastered the internet and have become completely at home with Skype; younger people who in spite of some serious disability have found the means to live a very full life that is marked by the service of others. The man in today's Gospel reading who approaches Jesus could well be the patron saint of all those who strive to connect with others against all the odds.

Unlike the leper, Jesus was perfectly healthy; yet like the leper, he had something of the same desire and energy to connect with others. When Jesus was approached by the leper, he could have run away, as most people would have. Instead, he stood his ground and engaged with the leper. He not only spoke to the leper, but he touched him. Jesus often healed people by means of his word alone; but this man who had suffered from extreme isolation needed to be touched. Jesus did more than was asked of him; he took an initiative that was as daring as the leper's initiative towards him. He went as far as any human being could possibly go to deliver this man from his isolation. What the Lord did for the leper he wishes to continue doing through each one of us in our own day. There are many isolated and lonely people among us. The scope is there for all of us to take the kind of step that Jesus took towards the leper. There are many examples in every parish community, such as people who look in on neighbours and make sure that they are all right and have what they need. There are always people among us waiting to be touched by our compassionate presence. When they are, they can experience the same kind of transformation as the leper did in today's Gospel reading.

Seventh Sunday in Ordinary Time

Carrying and being carried

Is 43:18-19, 21-2, 24-5; 2 Cor 1:18-22; Mk 2:1-12

You can think that you are familiar with a building because you have frequented it so often, but then suddenly you see something as if for the first time. A few years ago, I discovered a part of our church building I had never much noticed. Just beyond the main wall of the church, there was a small enclosed area with no roof over it. It was open to the elements and there were bits of vegetation growing there. You entered this space through a wooden door that was unlocked. The space used to be a boiler house. There is something rather sad about a four-sided space with no roof. The space has since been refurbished as a badly needed storage room. When a building loses its roof, the space underneath is gradually reclaimed by nature. When there is a problem with the roof of our house or our premises we tend to take immediate action, because we know the consequences of taking no action.

In today's Gospel reading, four friends of a paralysed man do serious damage to a roof of a house in order to get their friend as close to Jesus as possible. It is an extraordinary image. There is Jesus preaching to what was literally a full house when suddenly an opening starts to appear in the roof above, that gradually gets bigger until it was big enough to allow a paralysed man to be lowered in front of Jesus. The energy of those men who tore away at that roof was the energy of faith and the energy of love, faith in Jesus and love for their friend. I am reminded of a verse in Paul's letter to the Galatians, where Paul says, 'The only thing that counts is faith working through love.' Here indeed was a case of faith working through love. Rather than taking exception to this rather unorthodox entrance, Jesus recognised the source of the energy behind it. 'Seeing their faith, Jesus said to the paralytic …' Jesus recognised the faith of his friends. Nothing is said about the faith of the paralytic. It was the faith of his friends that carried the paralytic to Jesus and that created a space where Jesus could minister to him.

There is a wonderful image here of what the Church is about. We are all called to bring each other to the Lord. There are times in our lives when we can't make it to the Lord on our own. Perhaps we just don't have the faith; our faith has grown weak; we sense a certain paralysis of the spirit. We need people of faith to carry us to the Lord. We need to be carried along by the energy of other people's faith and the energy of the love that springs from their faith. That energy of faith and love may find expression in prayer on our behalf. We may not be able to pray, but we know that people are praying for us. Their faith and love which finds expression in their prayer for us somehow touches our lives and creates a space for the Lord to work in our lives. The energy of the faith and love of others may also find expression in practical action on our behalf, the kind of action displayed by the friends of the paralytic, action that brings us to a place we could not get to ourselves, a place where the Lord can touch our lives in a new way. The journey towards physical and spiritual healing often begins with the support given to us through the faith and the love of others.

At different times in our lives we can find ourselves either in the position of the paralytic or in the position of the friends of the paralytic. There are times when we need people of faith to carry us, when we desperately need the support of the community of faith. We can find that support sometimes by coming into a church building like this where people of faith gather. We may stumble in here without any strong sense that we really want to be here, wondering perhaps why we came or what we are doing here. To our surprise we may find that the faith of the community gathered for worship touches us in some way. The Lord touches us through the faith of those gathered. Without my appearing to do anything much, I find myself graced in some way. I come in my poverty and to my surprise I receive. There are other times when my faith is strong and it gives me the energy to carry others in love. In ways that I am perhaps only dimly aware of, the Lord works through me to grace the lives of others. For all of us there is a time to give and a time to receive, a time to serve others with our love and faith and a time to be served by the faith and love of others.

Eighth Sunday in Ordinary Time   *The bridegroom's new wine*

Is 2:16–17, 21–2; 2 Cor 3:1–6; Mk 2:18–22

Weddings are wonderful celebratory events. People come together to celebrate the love of a couple who promise to give themselves to be faithful to each other all the days of their lives. The joy of the couple is infectious, transmitting itself to all their loved ones and friends.

In the Gospel reading, Jesus speaks of his public ministry as a wedding feast. He is the bridegroom and his disciples are the bridegroom's attendants. Elsewhere in the Gospels Jesus recognised his ministry in the children who wanted to play the pipes for other children to dance to. There was plenty of dancing at weddings in Jesus' day as there is in our own day. In the fourth Gospel, John the Baptist identifies himself as the friend of the bridegroom who rejoices greatly at the bridegroom's voice. If Jesus is the bridegroom, we might be tempted to ask, 'Who is the bride?' Saint Paul in his second letter to the Corinthians identifies the church in Corinth as Christ's bride, 'I promised you in marriage to one husband, to present you as a chaste virgin to Christ.' This draws on the language of the prophets in the Jewish scriptures who often spoke of the relationship between God and his people as that between a husband and his bride. In today's first reading, God addresses his people as a wife whom he is going to woo once again. God will lure his people into the wilderness where he will speak to their heart in love and evoke a loving response once more from them. This will make possible a new betrothal between God and his people wherein God will display his qualities of integrity, justice, tenderness, love and faithfulness.

Across the Gospels, Jesus uses several images to express the richness of this relationship with us. He is the good shepherd and we are his flock. He is the vine and we are the branches. He is the teacher and we are his pupils. He is the master and we are his servants. However, the image of the bridegroom and bride captures a quality in the Lord's relationship with us that the other images don't quite express to the same extent, and that is the quality of faithful and intimate love. The Lord wants to be as close to us as a husband is to his wife and desires for us to be as close to him as a wife is to her husband. The faithful love of husband and wife is a partial revelation of the depth of the Lord's faithfulness to us. He looks for a similar quality of faithfulness to him on our part in return. Perhaps the other image of the Lord's relationship to us that expresses the same quality of faithfulness and intimacy is that of friend. On one occasion, Jesus says to his disciples in the fourth Gospel, 'I call you friends.' A deep friendship between a man and a woman is a solid foundation for married love.

The image of the Lord as lover and friend can seem very attractive and appealing. We long for an experience of friendship and love that has our present and ultimate good at heart. We will find such an experience in our relationship with the Lord. Yet, the Lord's love and friendship has another, more challenging, side to it. In the Gospel reading, Jesus uses another image that is related to the image of the wedding banquet, namely, the image of wine. In the time and culture of Jesus, a wedding would not be a celebration without an abundance of wine. The account of the wedding feast of Cana in the fourth Gospel suggests the embarrassment of the couple when the wine runs out. Having spoken of his ministry as a wedding feast, Jesus goes on to speak of it as new wine. 'Nobody puts new wine into old wineskins ... New wine, new skins.' The wine that is being served at the wedding feast of Jesus' ministry has a quality of newness to it that took people by surprise. In response to the first miracle of Jesus in Mark's Gospel, people exclaimed, 'What is this? A new teaching with authority?' Because of the newness of Jesus' ministry, the religious authorities keep questioning Jesus, asking 'Why?' in these opening chapters of Mark, 'Why does this fellow speak in this way? Why does he eat with tax collectors and sinners?' and in today's Gospel reading, 'Why do John's disciples and the disciples of the Pharisees fast, but your disciples do not fast?' In the next passage the Pharisees will ask, 'Why are they (the disciples) doing what is not lawful on the Sabbath?'

The guardians of the old wine skins were finding the new wine of Jesus' ministry disturbing and unsettling. In the Gospel reading, Jesus calls for fresh skins. The dynamic power of God's kingdom at work through Jesus calls for new ways of thinking, imagining and behaving. The love of the bridegroom will never leave us completely comfortable in our own skin. What Paul calls in today's second reading the covenant of the Spirit will always require us to keep letting go and moving on. We can be tempted to hold on to the familiar when the Lord's love is inviting us to take a new step more in keeping with the dynamism of the Spirit that blows where it wills.

Ninth Sunday in Ordinary Time   *Genuine Sabbath rest*

Deut 5:12–15; 2 Cor 4:6–11; Mk 2:23–3:6

In all walks of life, timing can be vitally important. In sport, the timing of a pass can determine whether the ball ends up in the net or not. In disputes between groups or individuals, the timing of an intervention can determine whether the dispute is resolved or not. In family life and in all human relationships a timely word can have an impact for good, as indeed can a timely silence. The author of the Book of Qoheleth, one of the Wisdom books of the Jewish scriptures, writes, 'For everything there is a season, and a time for every matter under heaven.' One aspect of human wisdom is knowing the right time for everything.

The dispute between Jesus and the religious leaders in today's Gospel reading could be understood as one about timing. Jesus' hungry disciples fed themselves on ears of corn as they walked through a cornfield. The objection of the Pharisees was not to the action as such but to its timing, 'Why are they doing something on the Sabbath day that is forbidden?' In a synagogue, somewhere in Galilee, Jesus healed a man with a withered hand. Again, the objection of Jesus was not so much to what he did but to the timing of his action. He cured the man on the Sabbath day. The Pharisees considered both the actions of the disciples and of Jesus untimely. In contrast, Jesus considered both actions timely. Who was the wiser?

The Jewish Sabbath was a distinctive Jewish custom. According to the Book of Genesis, God rested from his work of creating the world on the seventh day. Israel understood that the seventh day of the week, or Sabbath, should be a day of rest for all of humanity, regardless of their social status, indeed, a day of rest for all of God's creatures. The Sabbath was a time to step back from the daily grind and to attend to God and to the wonder of his creation. There is a great value in the Jewish religious custom of the Sabbath. It carried over into Christianity, even though the Christian Sabbath was not the seventh day of the week but the first day of the week, the day on which Jesus rose from the dead. For Christians, the Sabbath is a day to attend to God and the wonder of his creation and also a day to attend to Jesus our risen Lord and the wonder of God's new creation in and through the death and Resurrection of his son. We have lost this sense of Sabbath. Sunday has become much like every other day. The need to recover Sabbath is all the greater in an age where the pace of life can be so relentless and where God can be so easily pushed to the margins.

Jesus was a Jew and had great respect for the Jewish Sabbath. The Ten Commandments, one of which was 'Observe the Sabbath day and keep it holy', were at the core of his attitude to life. The dispute Jesus had with the Pharisees related to the interpretation of that commandment. What is and what is not permitted on the Sabbath? The Pharisees had come to interpret the Sabbath law in a rather restrictive way. Perhaps their view of the Sabbath law could be expressed as, 'people are made for the Sabbath'. Jesus' view, as expressed in the Gospel reading, was rather, 'the Sabbath was made for people'. Jesus was declaring that religious law, including the Sabbath commandment, must always be at the service of people's well-being. If law is not serving human well-being, especially the well-being of the most vulnerable, then it has lost its validity. As the disciples were walking through the corn fields, they were hungry. They had every right to satisfy their hunger by picking ears of corn. An interpretation of the Sabbath law which leaves people hungry is contrary to God's purpose for humanity. When Jesus encountered a man with a withered hand in the synagogue on the Sabbath, he had every right to heal the man. An interpretation of the Sabbath law which deprives people of the opportunity to live a fuller life is contrary to God's purpose for humanity. Jesus is saying that it is

Journeying with Mark

always timely to feed the hungry and to heal the sick. When it comes to meeting people's basic needs, there is no forbidden time.

Jesus' more flexible understanding of the Sabbath law is in keeping with the interpretation of the Sabbath found in today's first reading. According to the Book of Deuteronomy, the Sabbath is the one day when everyone, slave and free man, can enjoy rest equally, in remembrance of God's liberating action in bringing his people out of the slavery of Egypt. The Sabbath is about recalling God's liberating love for suffering humanity. What better way of celebrating Sabbath, therefore, than by allowing the hungry to be fed and the broken to be healed? God's liberating work of enhancing human well-being is the work that is most appropriate on the Sabbath. Our Christian Sabbath is an opportunity for us not only to rest from our labours but to use our rest to serve the Lord present to us in the most vulnerable. A visit to a sick relative or a lonely grandparent is the kind of 'work' the Sabbath is there for.

Tenth Sunday in Ordinary Time

Jesus' new family

Gn 3:9-15; 2 Cor 4:13-5:1; Mk 3:20-35

Every so often a crisis arises in a family relating to a family member and other family members feel the need to intervene. It can be difficult to know whether or not it is a good thing to intervene. Will it make matters better or worse? If a decision is made to intervene, there arises the question as to how best to do so. Such interventions are not always well received by the family member, even if they are done out of love and concern, which is generally the motivation for acting.

We find a somewhat similar situation in the family of Jesus in today's Gospel reading. Since he left his home in Nazareth, Jesus has literally been a man with a mission. The son of the carpenter has become the proclaimer of the presence of God's kingdom. His message was experienced as good news by many, especially the most vulnerable and broken. However, the same message was perceived as dangerous and troublesome by others, especially those who prided themselves on understanding God's will as expressed in the Jewish law. Jesus has been making many enemies among the influential and the powerful. So much so that many people have been saying about Jesus, 'he is out of his mind'. Jesus' family feel the need to do something out of concern for his well-being. The beginning of today's Gospel reading says that his relatives set out from Nazareth to take charge of Jesus. It sounded as if they were going to forcibly take him home. The end of today's Gospel reading shows what happened when they reached the house in Capernaum where Jesus was teaching with a group of his followers sitting around him. When Jesus was informed that his family, including his mother, were outside asking for him to come out, he looked around at those seated about him and said, 'Here are my mother and brothers.' In effect, Jesus meant, 'This is now my family.' Everyone who seeks to do God's will as Jesus reveals it is now a member of his new family.

Here was a family intervention that did not quite go according to plan from the perspective of Jesus' family of origin. God was at work in the life of Jesus in a way that his family did not understand and struggled to accept. Their plans and purposes for Jesus were too small. They had yet to learn to surrender to God's purpose for Jesus' life. Sometimes our plans and purposes for others, even for those we love the best, can be too confining. We often struggle to let them go to a greater purpose that we don't fully understand at the time. God's purpose for Jesus was that he would form a new family, a family of his disciples. In time, this new family came to be called the Church. We are all members of that new family of Jesus. God's purpose for Jesus' life has come to embrace us all. All who have been baptised in the name of the Trinity belong to the family of the Church. The words of Jesus at the end of today's Gospel reading are very striking. He is saying in effect that the members of his blood family do not have a stronger claim to him by virtue of their blood relationship. He clearly wants the members of his family of origin to become members of his new family, but, in doing so they are no more his brothers and sisters and mother than the other members of his new family. Jesus' words bring home to us the privileged relationship we have with him. Through the Holy Spirit, we have become his brothers and sisters. Although he is the Son of God in a unique sense, we have been incorporated into Jesus' relationship with God, making us sons and daughters of God.

All of this is a great privilege, but it also entails a call. When Jesus looked around at his new family at the end of today's Gospel reading, he said, 'Anyone who does the will of God, that person is my brother and sister and mother.' The call to do the will of God, as Jesus has revealed it to us, does not always come easy to us. The first reading refers to Adam who followed his own will rather than God's will, eating from the tree that God had forbidden him, in an effort to be like God. As a result of not doing God's will, he felt distant from God and hid from God, so God had to cry out after him, 'Where are you?' In the Gospel reading, the learned scribes were clearly acting contrary to God's will in attributing Jesus' healing power to an evil spirit rather than to God's Spirit. Jesus declares that those who demonise goodness in this way put themselves beyond the reach of God's forgiveness. The demonising of those who proclaim God's will to the world, and live accordingly, tends to be a feature of all totalitarian regimes. As members of Jesus' family, Jesus taught us to pray, 'Thy will be done on earth, as it is in heaven.' Our daily calling is to seek to make that prayer a reality in the concrete circumstances of our lives.

Eleventh Sunday in Ordinary Time

Small and hidden can be powerful

Ez 17:22-4; 2 Cor 5:6-10; Mk 4:26-34

We are exposed to bad news a lot of the time. The media can overwhelm us with reports of wars, famines, violence and scandals, big and small. The incredible speed with which news spreads can add to the sense we feel of being overwhelmed by suffering and evil in its various forms. We can feel helpless and discouraged before it all. All of this bad news of course is an accurate picture of what is going on in our world. We cannot simply pretend it does not exist. We need to acknowledge all of this negativity and to name it. The media provides an important service in helping us to do just that. Yet, there is more going on in our world of a much more wholesome nature that does not always get the same publicity.

This is part of the message that comes through to us in today's Gospel reading, in which Jesus tells two parables to express the reality of the kingdom of God. We can be tempted to think of the kingdom of God as a place beyond this life. Yet, that is not what Jesus primarily meant by the term 'kingdom of God'. The 'kingdom of God' is more a way of life than a place. Whenever we live as God wants us to live, there the kingdom of God is present. Jesus was the person who fully lived in the way God wants us to live. God was pleased with everything that Jesus said and did. That is why everywhere Jesus went the kingdom of God was present. The first thing Jesus said when he started his mission was, 'the kingdom of God is here'. Whenever we live like Jesus, the kingdom of God is present. Jesus taught us to pray, 'Thy kingdom come, thy will be done, on earth as it is in heaven.' Whenever we do God's will, as revealed by Jesus, whenever we speak and act as God would want us to do, there the kingdom of God is at hand. Whenever we live out of the mindset of Jesus, there the kingdom of God is among us. Whenever we allow our lives to be shaped by the Holy Spirit, the kingdom of God is present.

In that first parable, Jesus compares the kingdom of God to a farmer who throws seed on the ground and, having done so, must step back and let nature takes its course. As he goes about his business, sleeping, waking, the seed is growing. Only when what was sown is ripe for harvest can the farmer really get to work again. Throughout this process, the farmer has a role to play, but nature has its own work to do in its own time. Jesus is saying that the kingdom of God, living in a way that is in keeping with God's will for our lives, is a bit like that. Yes, we have our work to do if that is to happen, just as the farmer had to sow the seed and then reap the harvest; however, there is something more going on all the time, apart from our work. The Lord himself is at work in our lives. It is not all down to us, just as it is not all down to the farmer. In his letter to the church in Philippi, Paul expresses his confidence that God who began a good work among them would bring it to completion. The work of growing into Christ, living out of the mindset of Christ, was primarily God's good work in their lives. The coming of the kingdom is God's good work in our lives. Our work consists primarily in cooperating with the work of God that is ongoing in our lives. Even in the midst of all the bad news that is around us, the good work of God continues in the lives of all those who are in any way open to that work of God within us and among us.

Jesus then uses a second seed parable to speak of the kingdom of God. He says it is like a mustard seed, the smallest of all the seeds, which once sown becomes a huge shrub putting out big branches. Jesus is saying that the kingdom of God is as present in the mustard seed as in the large shrub. Doing God's will, living as God wants us to live, following in the way of Jesus, is not necessarily about doing big things but it can also be about doing small things well. If we manage to sow little seeds of the kingdom, the Lord can work powerfully through those small seeds until they grow into something wonderful. We need to learn to appreciate the little efforts we make – a friendly gesture towards someone in trouble, a welcoming smile for someone who feels excluded, a sign of closeness for someone who is alone. In all these small ways, the mustard seed of the kingdom of God is at hand and it can grow into something wonderful. Faithful everyday choices to scatter the seed of the Lord's love will unleash a power that can transform the world.

Twelfth Sunday in Ordinary Time · *The Lord in the storm*

Job 3:1, 8-11; 2 Cor 5:14-17; Mk 4:35-41

We are fortunate to be so close to the sea in our parish. In good weather, it is lovely to live near the sea, especially when we have such a lovely promenade. Every year I take part in an ecumenical blessing of boats ceremony. We are blessed to have a relatively sheltered stretch of water between the promenade and the open sea where people can sail reasonably safely. It is a wonderful amenity. Yet, for all the attractiveness of the sea, we know that it can be treacherous. Even our sheltered stretch of water can sometimes look quite choppy, never mind the open sea beyond the lighthouse. Those who spend time on the sea learn to treat it with respect, because they know it can be a destructive force as well as a benign one.

The Sea of Galilee which features in today's Gospel reading is more a very large lake than a sea. Yet, because it is below sea level and surrounded by hills and valleys, winds can blow down the valleys and whip up the waters without much prior notice. Some of the disciples that were in the boat with Jesus were fishermen. They knew the lake well. When a storm broke on the lake, however, they were understandably filled with fear. Something of their panic is captured in the words they address to Jesus, 'Master, do you not care? We are going down.' The panic of the disciples stands in sharp contrast to the attitude of Jesus – 'in the stern, his head on a cushion, asleep'. The panic of the disciples revealed their anxiety that the chaos of the storm would overwhelm them; the sleep of Jesus indicated his deep conviction that all would be well. Different people can react to crises in different ways. Some remain calm and others go to pieces. In a crisis, we need at least some people to remain calm and to have a calming influence on everybody else.

Mark's Gospel was probably written to the Church in Rome about the year 70 AD. This was a church that had gone through very stormy times. It had experienced the trauma of Nero's persecution, and, in the process, had lost many of its key leaders, such as Peter and Paul. As the members of the Church tried to come to terms with their bruising experience, some of them may have been wondering, 'Where is the risen Lord in all of this? Has he abandoned us? Is he asleep to what is happening to us?' In including this incident in his Gospel, Mark was trying to assure his church that as Jesus was in the boat with the disciples when the storm broke, he was now with the Church in its ordeal. The members of the Church in Rome were being asked to put their faith in the Lord in the midst of the storm and to trust that the Lord is stronger than the storm. The disciples of Mark's own day were being invited to reflect on the question of the disciples in the boat, 'Who can this be?' and then, in the light of the Gospel reading, to give the answer, 'Jesus is the one who brings order out of chaos, life out of death.'

This is also the answer that we, the Church today, are being asked to give to this question. We may not have to contend with a Nero, at least not in most parts of the world, but no one can deny that the Church has been through very stormy times, with some of the storms of the Church's own making. Recent decades have been disheartening for many believers. In Western Europe at least, the Church appears to be in a period of decline. The waves of secularism and materialism threaten to sink the Church, which has often been understood as the ship of Peter. Such storms, however, can have their own cathartic effect; they can work to renew and purify the Church. The disciples in today's Gospel reading undoubtedly learned something important from their traumatic experience with the storm on the Sea of Galilee. The storm made them question more deeply, 'Who then is this?' Stormy times can help us all to question more deeply and, in the process, to recover some basics. A weakened, vulnerable Church can come to recognise in a new way its total dependence on the Lord. When all is not well, we often seek the Lord with greater passion, like the disciples in the boat, rather than presuming that we already know him. In that way, difficult and painful times can deepen the Church's relationship with the Lord.

In today's second reading, St Paul reflects on the relationship between the Lord and the Church. He declares that Christ died for all, so that we might live no longer for ourselves but for him. He died for all so that we who believe might live for him. We who are the Church do not live for ourselves, but for the Lord. The Church exists to serve the Lord, not to serve itself. The storms through which the Church passes can help it to reappropriate this fundamental truth.

Thirteenth Sunday in Ordinary Time   *Faith in the face of loss*

Wis 1:13–15; 2:23–4; 2 Cor 8:7, 9, 13–15; Mk 5:21–43

One of the greatest of human sufferings is for a parent to lose a child. There can be nothing more devastating. The emotional pain involved is like no other. Those who try to journey with parents in the face of such a devastating loss struggle to know how to accompany them. They know that there are no words that can bring consolation. There is a sense of helplessness that is shared by everybody. If the parents are people of faith, their faith can be shaken to the core, as is the faith of those who are trying to journey with them. We cannot help asking the question, 'Why did God allow this to happen? Where is God in the midst of this terrible loss and pain?' The bond between a parent and a son or daughter is so deep and profound that when the son or daughter suffers, the parent suffers equally and if the son or daughter dies, something dies in the parent. A parent will move heaven and earth to prevent this from happening. Parental love is a unique kind of love; it is all absorbing and overrides every other consideration. In a very literal sense, parents live for their children, because when they look upon their child, they are looking upon themselves, bone of their bone and flesh of their flesh.

We find a powerful expression of such parental love in today's Gospel reading. Jairus was a synagogue official, the father of a seriously ill girl aged twelve. We are told that he fell at Jesus' feet, pleading with him earnestly. For a man of his social standing to fall at the feet of a travelling prophet would have involved a loss of honour and dignity on his part. However, such considerations were irrelevant at a time like this. He pleaded that Jesus come to his home and Jesus responded. Yet, as Jesus was on his way, he was delayed by someone else's need and before he got to the house the terrible news came through to Jairus, 'your daughter is dead'. This is the devastating, world-shattering news that no parent should ever have to hear. Those who brought this news to Jairus told him not to trouble Jesus anymore. Now that the young girl was dead, Jesus had no further role to play. It seemed to be reasonable advice. Perhaps that advice reflects how parents feel when they hear similarly awful news. 'Why continue to relate to the Lord? He has failed us. Why bother with him?' Even those of us who have had to cope with less serious losses than a parent's loss of a child can find ourselves asking the same questions. Yet, it was precisely at this very moment, when the reasons for trusting had been taking away, that Jesus says to Jairus, 'Do not be afraid. Only have faith.'

Jesus called upon Jairus to have faith in the face of his daughter's death. The Lord continues to call out to us to keep faith even in the face of a death that seems to make no human sense. The Gospel reading tells us that when Jesus reached Jairus' home, he took his daughter by the hand and brought her back from death to life and ordered that food be given to her. This was not the experience of many other parents who lost children in the time and place of Jesus. It is not the experience of parents today who lose a child in the way Jairus did. Yet, this incident in the life of Jesus was recorded in our Gospels because it was recognised that it had something important to say to believers of every generation. The Lord's words to Jairus are intended for all of us: 'Do not be afraid. Only have faith.' We are being reminded that Jesus can and will bring new life out of our many deaths, including those deaths that leave us devastated. That new life is ultimately a sharing in the Lord's own risen life.

The story of Jairus frames another story in our Gospel reading, the story of a woman who displays the kind of faith that Jesus called on Jairus to have and calls on all of us to have. She too had to come to terms with great loss. Because of her physical condition, she would have been considered ritually unclean in that culture, in the way that lepers were; she was an outcast. Not only had she lost all her finances, but she had lost her community. However, she hadn't lost her faith. She found her own way to Jesus, a way that was very personal to her, and unknown to everyone else. Yet, her way of touching Jesus in faith was not unknown to him. He called her forth from the crowd so that she could witness to her faith before others. When she did so, Jesus addressed her as 'my daughter'. This woman models for us a faith that endures in the face of all the odds, a faith that brings us into a deeply personal relationship with Jesus, even in the midst of loss, a faith that opens us up to the Lord's life-giving presence in this earthly life and beyond it.

Fourteenth Sunday in Ordinary Time   *God in failure*

Ez 2:2–5; 2 Cor 12:7–10; Mk 6:1–6

We live in an age that values success. As a result, failure can be very hard to accept and to deal with. Yet, it is an inevitable part of human experience. We cannot go through life without failing at something. We might set out on a certain path and we don't reach the destination we had hoped for, in spite of our best efforts. We put a great deal of time and energy into some enterprise and the result is not what we would have wanted. Perhaps the most painful experience of failure relates to the breakdown of some relationship that had been very significant for us. Such experiences can leave us discouraged, disheartened, lacking the energy to begin again and to keep going.

Today's readings reflect that experience of failure. Jesus' mission in his hometown of Nazareth appears to have been a total failure. He left Nazareth to go down to the Jordan river where John the Baptist had been baptising. After his Baptism and a period of forty days in the wilderness where he was put to the test, he began his public ministry, preaching, teaching and healing in the towns and villages of Galilee. He met with opposition from the religious leaders, but he drew huge crowds of the people to himself, especially the broken, the excluded, the lost. He must have gone to Nazareth with a certain expectation that he would be well received in his own place. He preached in their synagogue on the Sabbath day, as he had done in the other synagogues of Galilee. However, the response to him was one of cold indifference, even hostility. The townspeople presumed they knew him; he is the carpenter, the son of Mary. Once a carpenter, always a carpenter. Who does he think he is, speaking and acting above his station? The Gospel reading makes a striking statement, 'Jesus could work no miracles there.' He simply couldn't function among his own townspeople and relations. He was disempowered by their refusal to take him seriously.

Even Jesus was powerless before people's lack of openness. This experience of failure must have come as a bitter disappointment to him. Yet, it was only a foretaste of the much more painful experience of failure he would have to endure in the city of Jerusalem. He was despised in Nazareth; he would be crucified in Jerusalem.

Jesus drank the bitter cup of failure. I came across a sentence in a book recently which spoke strongly to me: 'God dealt with our failure by becoming a failure and dealing with it from the inside. This is why we can meet God in our failure.' God became a failure on Calvary, in the person of his crucified son. There was no greater proclamation of failure in the world of Jesus than the act of crucifixion. Because God has plumbed the darkest depths of human failure, we can meet God in our own experiences of failure. Those experiences of life that bring home to us our limitations, our weaknesses, our powerlessness are not the dead ends they often appear to be. The Lord is powerfully with us in those moments, working to bring something new out of what seems very unpromising. That was the experience of Paul in today's second reading. He speaks about a 'thorn in the flesh' that he was given. We cannot be sure what he means by this phrase, but it was obviously some painful experience that he could see no good in. That is why he refers to it as 'an angel of Satan'. It came into the category of failure. It was an obstacle that prevented him from doing God's work successfully. Paul speaks of it as an expression of his 'weakness'. He pleaded with God to be free of it, in the expectation that his prayer would be heard. His prayer was heard but not in the way that he expected. He was left with this thorn in the flesh, but it was revealed to him in prayer that the Lord was working powerfully in and through this thorn, from which Paul so desperately wanted to be free. He heard the Lord say to him, 'My grace is enough for you. My power is at its best in weakness.' The very experience that he saw as of no value, as pure negativity, was where the Lord was most powerfully present. It was as if Paul came to see that just as God was powerfully present in the failure of Christ on the cross, so he was powerfully present through what Paul recognised as his failures, his powerlessness.

When we come face to face in our own lives with failure, loss, rejection, we often need to stand back so as to see these painful experiences with the eyes of faith, rather than just with the eyes of our culture, the eyes of the world. We reflect on these experiences with the conviction that the Lord may be powerfully present here in a life-giving way. We face our failures, our weaknesses, our brokenness, with hope, recognising, with St Paul, that the Lord's power is always at work somewhere in our weakness.

Fifteenth Sunday in Ordinary Time

Journeying in response to a call

Am 7:12-15; Eph 1:3-14; Mk 6:7-13

July and August are traditionally the months when people take holidays. More often than not, we speak in terms of going away on holiday. For most of us, a holiday involves a going, a setting out on a journey of some kind. An important part of a holiday is leaving the familiar, the place where we usually live and work, and heading off to a different place. There is always something exciting about setting out on such a journey. We make such a journey gladly and willingly, with a sense of expectation and anticipation. Such journeys are of our own choosing; we make them because we want to make them.

There are other journeys in life that are not of our choosing in quite the same way. These are journeys we make because, at some level, we feel we must make them. Something deep within us moves us to take a certain path, to head out in a certain direction. Even though we sense the journey may be difficult, and we may have all kinds of hesitations and reservations about it, nonetheless, we know we must set out on this path if we are to be true to our values. Yes, we choose to make such a journey, but it is a choice in response to what seems like a call from beyond ourselves or from deep within ourselves.

Such a journey is put before us in today's first reading. Amos was a shepherd and a dresser of sycamore trees in the southern kingdom of Judah. Yet, at a certain moment in his life, he felt a compulsion to make a difficult journey into the northern kingdom of Israel to preach the word of God there. It was a most unlikely journey for the likes of Amos to make, and Amos was well aware it would be no holiday. Yet, he also knew that this was a journey he simply had to make. He spoke of the compulsion he felt in terms of God's call, 'The Lord ... took me from herding the flock and ... said "Go". Amos went because he had a strong sense that he was being sent by God. In a similar way, in the Gospel reading, the disciples set out on a journey because they are sent on that journey by Jesus. They set out freely, but in response to a call, a sending.

The experience of Amos and the disciples is also very often our experience. Like them, we can find ourselves setting out on a journey that is not completely of our choosing. In today's second reading Paul speaks about the mystery of God's purpose. God has a purpose for our lives. That same reading speaks about God's choice. God has chosen us to live in a certain way, chosen us to live and to journey as Jesus did. Although we are constantly making all kinds of journeys of our own choosing, whether it is the journey associated with a holiday or some other journey, there is a more fundamental journey that God has chosen for us. God's choice, God's purpose, impinges on us throughout our lives, prompting us to take certain paths and to avoid others, moving us to set out in one direction rather than another. The basic shape of the journey that God has chosen for us is visible in the life of Jesus. God never ceases to call us to take that journey, to walk in the way of his son. Although God has chosen this journey for us, 'before the world was made', according to the second reading, God also wants us to choose this journey for ourselves, and God waits for us to do so. This is not a choice we make once and for all. Rather, it is a choice we are constantly remaking. Throughout our lives, we keep on choosing to surrender to God's purpose for our lives. We keep on trying to set out on the journey God is calling us to take, we keep on inviting God to have his way in our lives, saying with Mary, 'Let it be to me according to your word.'

If we keep on choosing the journey that God has chosen for us in Christ, responding to God's call, this will impact on all the various smaller journeys we take in life. It will influence the way we holiday, for example. We will choose to holiday in ways that are genuinely recreational, that truly recreate us in the image of God's son. We will relax in ways that are life-giving for ourselves and for others, that help us to become more fully the person God has chosen us to be.

The readings today invite us to become more attuned to the Lord's call to journey in a particular way. Like Amos and the disciples, we may feel anxious before this call, but in heeding that call, we are assured of what the second reading refers to as 'the richness of the grace that God has showered upon us.' The Lord does not send us out on the journey he has chosen for us without also providing for us along the way. As we try to be faithful to the Lord's way, we will experience, in the words of today's psalm, the Lord's saving help.

Sixteenth Sunday in Ordinary Time   *God in the interruptions*

Jer 23:1-6; Eph 2:13-18; Mk 6:30-4

We are very much in the middle of holiday time. Many people are about to go on holidays, have just come back from holidays or are away on holidays. We all need a break from our routine, whatever that routine might be. Most of the time we go on holidays with somebody, or we go away to stay with somebody. Most of us like to be with others when we are away from our routine. In the Gospel reading we find Jesus taking his disciples away together for a period of rest and quiet. They have had a busy time of mission; they were full of all they had done and taught and wanted to share it all with Jesus. He reacted by suggesting a change of pace and of location. He intended to take them away to a lonely place, a desert place, where they could rest. This was to be a time of reflection in the company of Jesus, a time when they did nothing except be present to each other and to the Lord.

In our own lives we all need such desert moments, times when we try to be present to the Lord and to each other. We have a prayer group in the parish that meets on a Monday night; it is a desert moment, a short period of about thirty minutes when people sit in silence having listened to a short talk. We have another prayer group that meets on a Tuesday evening, when a group of people gather around the Gospel reading for the following Sunday, and listen to it in silence and then share a little on how it has spoken to them. These are times when people are present to the Lord and to each other in a more intense way than is usually the case. They are little desert moments that people can share together, times when we can come away to rest for a while in the Lord's presence and in the presence of other believers. Our parish church is that sort of desert space in the middle of the community. It is a place to which people can come away and rest for a while, in the words of the Gospel reading. The silence can be an opportunity to share with the Lord what has been going on in our lives, just as in the Gospel reading the disciples shared with Jesus all they had been doing and teaching. Other people can have that desert moment as they walk along and enjoy the wonders of nature. As we walk we can become aware of the Lord and his presence among us, and we can become more aware of people in our lives, even though we may be walking alone. Whatever form it might take, as believers and followers of the Lord, we all need to come away to some lonely place all by ourselves and rest for a while, to allow the Lord to be in a deeper communion with us.

If the first part of the Gospel reading proclaims that value of coming away to be present to the Lord, the second part of the Gospel reading proclaims another value. The lonely place that the Lord and his disciples sought out suddenly became a crowded place, even before Jesus and his disciples arrived. They stepped out of the boat not into quietness and peace, but into human need and demand. We are all familiar with that kind of experience, aren't we? We plan something and it doesn't work out. We go somewhere expecting something and the opposite transpires. We want to be alone and we are inundated with people. Jesus and his disciples experienced a major interruption to what they were intending. Interruptions are part of all our lives, and as one writer put it, God is often to be found in the interruptions. Jesus responded to the interruption by become completely present to it. He did not try to avoid the crowd or to send them away; he attended to them fully. In the words of the Gospel reading, 'he took pity on them', 'he had compassion for them'. That is very much at the heart of our own calling as the Lord's followers; to be present to others, even when they turn up unexpectedly and interrupt what we had carefully planned. It is so easy to get worked up and irritated when something happens that is not part of the script we had in our head. We can be so fixed on that script that we can look on people as nuisances instead of being present to them with the compassion of Jesus. Jesus had the habit of spending time alone with God; it was those times of presence with God in prayer that enabled Jesus to be present to others, no matter who they were or how they turned up. Our own coming away to be with the Lord will help us too to be present to those who come into our lives. Our contemplative moments, our desert times, help us to be contemplative and attentive in relating to those who cross our path in life.

Seventeenth Sunday in Ordinary Time

The power of a small boy's gift

1 Kgs 4:42-4; Eph 4:1-6; Jn 6:1-15

We can sometimes find ourselves in a situation that seems beyond us. The gap between the resources we have at our disposal and the issue that is crying out to be addressed seems too great. We feel a sense of helplessness that drains us of the energy to tackle the problem. The challenge seems too demanding, in comparison to the resources we have at our disposal.

In today's Gospel reading we have an example of that kind of powerlessness before a daunting task. Jesus and the disciples are faced with a very large crowd of hungry people in a deserted place. They need to be fed and the resources to feed them don't appear to be there. The sense of being overwhelmed by the task at hand is audible in the comments that Jesus' disciples make. Philip states, 'Two hundred denarii would only buy enough to give them a small piece each.' Andrew comments that there is a small boy present with five barley loaves and two fish, but he asks rather despairingly, 'What is that between so many?' I am sure that people who work for aid agencies often found themselves in a similar situation in those parts of the world ravaged by conflict and famine. The huge need outstrips the available resources. Yet, in that situation such workers always do whatever they can with whatever resources they have at their disposal. They don't despair; they tackle the situation as best as they can.

In the Gospel reading, Jesus was just as aware as his disciples of the enormity of the task and the apparent lack of resources; however, he did not share their sense of defeatism. He saw that in some way the small boy with the five barley loaves and two fish was the key to feeding the vast crowd. We cannot be certain what exactly happened on that day in the wilderness but it seems certain that the small boy with his few barley loaves and fish played a very important role. There was only enough food there for a simple meal for a poor family. Yet, he was willing to part with his barley loaves and fish; he handed them over to Jesus and, in some mysterious way, Jesus was able to work with the young boy's generous gift to feed everyone. One generous boy was the beginning of the feeding of the multitude. The boy's generosity gave Jesus the opening that he needed. In and through this small boy's simple gift, Jesus worked powerfully.

This is one of the very few stories about Jesus that is to be found in all four Gospels. It clearly spoke very powerfully to the Early Church. Perhaps in and through this story the early believers came to appreciate that the Lord can use our tiniest efforts to perform his greatest works. As Paul declared in his letter to the Church in Corinth, God's power is often made perfect in our weakness. The Lord can work powerfully in and through the very little that we possess, if we are generous with that little. The small boy is our teacher in that regard. He gave over his few barley loaves and fish, and the Lord did the rest. So often the spontaneous generosity of children can have a great deal to teach us. In giving away the little we have we leave ourselves very vulnerable. Yet, the Gospel reading suggests that the Lord can work powerfully in and through that very vulnerability which is the fruit of our generosity. The Lord needs us to be generous with what we have, even though it can seem very small and very inadequate in our eyes. The Lord does not work in a vacuum; he needs us to create an opening for him to work. Without the presence of Jesus, the crowd would not have been fed. Without the presence of the small boy and his few resources, the crowd would not have been fed either. The Lord needs us to be generous with what we have today if he is to continue to feed the various hungers of today's crowd, whether it is the basic hunger for food, or the hunger for shelter, for a home, for friendship, for community, for acceptance or the deeper spiritual hunger for God.

The Gospel reading teaches us never to underestimate the significance of even the tiniest efforts we make to be generous with the resources we have at our disposal, whether it is resources of money, or time or some ability or other.

All four evangelists saw a connection between what happened in the wilderness on that day and what happened at the Last Supper and what happens at every Eucharist. Just as Jesus transformed the small boy's simple gifts of five barley loaves and two fish into a feast for thousands, so he transforms our simple gifts of bread and wine into a spiritual feast for all, the bread of life and the cup of salvation. The way the Lord works in the Eucharist is how he works in the rest of our lives. He takes the little we offer to him and by means of it, in the words of St Paul, he is 'able to accomplish abundantly far more than all we can ask or imagine'.

Eighteenth Sunday in Ordinary Time
Deeper hungers and thirsts

Ex 16:2-4; Eph 4:17, 20-4; Jn 6:24-35

There can come a time when we recognise that we are living our lives at a certain level and we feel a call to go to a deeper level in some way. I may be doing the usual things well but I sense that there is something more that I am being called to. In today's Gospel reading, the crowd who had been fed in the wilderness by Jesus with bread and fish a short time before come looking for Jesus. They want him to keep doing what he had just done, providing them with food. They go looking for him to get more of the same from him. They recognise him as someone who can provide for their basic physical needs. They are very much fixed at the level of the material and the physical.

When they find Jesus, he doesn't respond to their request for more of the same but invites them to go to a deeper level. 'Do not work for food that cannot last', he says, 'but work for food that endures to eternal life.' Jesus took food that cannot last very seriously. He fed the hungry and, indeed, identified himself with the hungry, 'I was hungry and you gave me something to eat.' He spoke a parable against the self-indulgent rich who were blind to the starving Lazarus at their gate. Jesus insisted that the basic physical needs of people be met by those who had more than they needed. He insisted that until this happens the kingdom of God will not have fully come. Yet, he was also very concerned with the deeper hungers and thirsts of people, their hunger for an unconditional love, for a forgiveness with no strings attached, for an experience of community where they would be valued not for what they possessed or their status but for who they were as human beings, for a healing that embraced their body, soul and spirit. It is to these deeper hungers of the human heart that Jesus speaks in today's Gospel reading when he says, 'I am the bread of life. Whoever comes to me will never be hungry; whoever believes in me will never thirst.'

When we hear Jesus refer to himself as the 'Bread of Life', we tend to think immediately of the Eucharist. The children who prepare for their first holy communion are taught that Jesus will be coming to them as the Bread of Life. All of this is true. Yet, in claiming to be the Bread of Life, Jesus is also making the very bold claim that he alone can satisfy those deeper hungers and thirsts of the human heart with which we are born and which never leave us, even though we can lose touch with them. Many people experience a kind of spiritual awakening at some point in their lives. They may have been very successful and accomplished at all sorts of levels and yet sense that there is some deeper level that they have never really attended to. They are aware of a deeper hunger that hasn't really been satisfied. The Lord is always offering us spiritual food but we don't always have much of an appetite for it. We can take it or leave it. Then something can happen that puts us in touch with some deeper hunger within us that has not been satisfied. Jesus offers himself to us in the Gospel reading as the one who can feed that deeper hunger.

When Jesus called on the people in today's Gospel reading to 'work for food that endures for eternal life', they responded by asking him what kind of work is involved, 'What are the works of God you are asking us to do?' Jesus replies by stating that there is only one work necessary, to believe in the one that God has sent. It is a faith relationship with Jesus that allows us to experience him as the Bread of Life who satisfies our deepest hunger. The question of the crowd, 'What work do we have to do to find this food that endures to eternal life?' is understandable. 'Tell us what to do' is their request. Jesus is saying that there is something more fundamental required than doing and that is being in a faith relationship with him. The Christian life does not consist primarily in faithfully complying with a list of practices and observances. Rather, at the heart of our identity as Christians is a living and trustful relationship with Jesus. All that God wants is that we believe in his son, because he is the great gift God has sent to the world in response to our deepest longings. This is what we need to work at, growing in our relationship with the Lord. All the rest will flow from this personal relationship. Such a relationship will bear fruit in all kinds of good works. This relationship, while personal, is not private. We must come together with other believers if we are to grow in our relationship with the Lord. It is in and through the community of believers, the Church, that we experience the Lord offering himself to us as the Bread of Life and that we respond to his wonderful offer.

Nineteenth Sunday in Ordinary Time

Bread in the wilderness

1 Kgs 19:4–8; Eph 4:20–5:2; Jn 6:41–51

People of faith often say that they are angry with God when they have been hit with something that leaves them broken and drained. It might be an experience of illness which affects either themselves or a loved one, or some deep loss after the sudden death of a loved one. All sorts of dark and painful experiences can leave us feeling that God has abandoned us. We may feel that we have served God well and that God has let us down. We can barely face God in prayer. We struggle to go to church and, especially, to Mass. People of faith have always had these dark emotions towards God. Many of the psalms are prayers out of the depths of some dark experience that often reveal anger and confusion.

We find an example of such a prayer at the beginning of today's first reading, on the lips of the great prophet, Elijah. He went into the wilderness and prayed, 'Lord, I have had enough. Take my life.' Elijah is often portrayed in the scriptures as the strong, fiery prophet, whose witness of God's word made him powerful enemies. Yet, in our reading today, we find Elijah at a very vulnerable moment of his life. Everything is going against him. He is having a crisis of faith. The life has been drained out of him. All he wants to do is sleep. Even more preferable to sleep would be death. Yet, he does not keep these dark moods to himself. He speaks out of his inner darkness to God, even though it meant speaking to God in anger, expressing his deep disappointment with God. Prayer does not have to be polite. Genuine prayer is always real; it is always true to who we are. Elijah's angry prayer kept the lines of communication to God open. In response to his heart-felt prayer, an angel of God touched him and invited him to get up and to eat. Elijah responded to this invitation, but promptly went back to sleep again. God was touching Elijah's spirit but his mood was not going to change quickly. A further visit from one of God's messengers, a further invitation to get up and eat, a further response from Elijah and he was finally on his feet once more and ready to face the journey that lay ahead.

We can all find ourselves in a similar situation to Elijah at some point in our lives. Life has a way of knocking the stuffing out of us, whether it is something distressing that happens to us or the way someone treats us or the sense we might have of our own personal failure. A withdrawal from life, in one form of another, can seem a tempting option. Today's first reading reminds us that when we are in that wilderness space, we do not have to struggle alone. The Lord is with us, and we can turn to him even if it is in our anger and despair. If we share our darkness with the Lord, we will be opening ourselves up to the light of his sustaining love. Like Elijah, we can come to discover that his angel, his messenger, comes to us in our need, very often in the most ordinary of ways, such as a phone call, a visit from someone, an invitation to a meal or a cup of coffee. The Lord will not leave us alone; he will provide for us.

The Lord is especially present to us in and through the community of believers, the Church. When we are at our lowest ebb, we need to put ourselves in the way of that community, even though that may be the very time when, in our anger, we are tempted to walk away. In the first reading, Elijah is told to get up and eat. In the Gospel reading, Jesus declares himself to be the Bread of Life, the living bread come down from heaven. He wants to give us life; he is bread broken for a broken people. He comes to us as the Bread of Life in and through the community of believers especially when we gather to listen to his word and to receive the Eucharist. The power of the community of faith to sustain us in our wilderness moments is powerfully expressed through a story shared by Francis Xavier Nguyen Van Thuan, who was once archbishop of Ho Chi Minh City. For thirteen years he was imprisoned in North Vietnam, spending nine of those years in solitary confinement. On one occasion a copy of the New Testament was smuggled into the prison for all the Catholic prisoners. So that they could all share this gift of the Lord's word, this Bread of Life, they ripped it into little sheets that were then distributed to everyone and each one memorised their sheet by heart. Every sunset, the prisoners took it in turn to recite aloud the part they had memorised. Van Thuan recalled that it was so moving to hear the word of God in the silence and the darkness, recited with such strength of faith. No one could doubt the presence of the Lord in the bread of his word feeding this little community of believers in their wilderness time.

Twentieth Sunday in Ordinary Time

A banquet of life and love

Prov 9:1–6; Eph 5:15–20; Jn 6:51–8

After people have moved into a new house or do some refurbishment on their home, they often have a little celebration in the house to which they invite people. Once the house is ready to their satisfaction they open it up to others and provide some refreshments. We often call it a house-warming. It is as if the house needs a good presence of other people to be properly launched. When you look at today's first reading you find something similar happening. We have this woman by the name of Wisdom. She builds herself a house, clearly a very elegant house; it has no less than seven pillars. She then throws a feast of fine wine and good meat and sends out her maid servants into the streets to gather people to her table. In that reading the building of a house, the making of a feast, the invitation to come and eat and drink, is an imaginative way of speaking about God as the wise host who invites all of humanity to learn from his wisdom. It is interesting that God is portrayed as a woman in this reading, Woman Wisdom.

That image of Woman Wisdom who says, 'Come and eat of my bread, drink the wine I have prepared' finds an echo in the figure of Jesus in the Gospel reading who declares, 'I am the living bread which has come down from heaven. Anyone who eats this bread will live forever.' Like Woman Wisdom, Jesus invites us to come and eat of his bread, but, unlike Woman Wisdom, he declares himself to be that bread. We are to eat of him, to drink of him. More specifically he calls on us to eat his flesh and to drink his blood. This goes far beyond anything Woman Wisdom calls for in that first reading. Jesus' language of eating his flesh and drinking his blood is shocking in many respects. We can sympathise with those who object, 'How can this man give us his flesh to eat?' We cannot hear this language without thinking of the words of Jesus to his disciples at the last supper when, taking bread, blessing it and breaking it, he gave it to them saying, 'Take, eat, this is my body', and taking and blessing a cup of wine he gave it to them, saying, 'Take, drink, this is the new covenant in my blood.' He gave himself to his disciples, his body and blood, under the form of bread and wine. The last supper became the first Eucharist. We cannot but hear the language of the Eucharist in today's Gospel reading, the Eucharist which we are now celebrating together.

We invite people to our home and we place food and drink before them and we invite them to eat and drink. Jesus invites us to his table and he puts himself before us as food and drink and invites us to eat and drink. In language that is very daring, Jesus declares himself to be our food and drink, the one who can satisfy our deepest hungers and thirsts, our hunger and thirst for life. Jesus declares in that Gospel reading, 'Anyone who eats my flesh and drinks my blood has eternal life.' We tend to think of 'eternal life' as a life that only begins after death. Yet, it is clear from the Gospel reading that by 'eternal life' Jesus does not just mean a life that begins after this earthly life ends. He understands eternal life as a life that we can begin to experience in the midst of this earthly life. That is why he says in that Gospel reading, 'As I, who am sent by the living Father, myself draw life from the Father, so whoever eats me will draw life from me.' Just as during his earthly life Jesus drew life from God, so during our earthly lives we can draw life from Jesus through our communion with him in the Eucharist. The life Jesus drew from God and we draw from Jesus is eternal; it is the life of God. Here and now through our communion with Jesus in the Eucharist we can enjoy a first taste of eternal life. What is eternal life only the life of God, the life of love, of a love that is unconditional and eternal? It is that life which we begin to taste in the Eucharist, because the Eucharist is the celebration of God's love for us in Christ. In the Eucharist God's loving gift of his son is made present over and over again. God so loved the world that he gave his only son.

We come to the Eucharist to draw life from the risen Lord, to draw God's life from him, God's love. We are then sent from the Eucharist to be channels of that life, of that love, for each other. We come to the Eucharist hungering and thirsting for life, for authentic life, the life of God, the love of God. We are sent out from the Eucharist as life-givers, as agents of God's life and love within our homes, our society, our world.

Twenty-First Sunday in Ordinary Time

Choosing the Lord and his gift

Jos 21:1-2, 15-18; Eph 5:21-32; Jn 6:60-9

Terry Anderson was an American journalist who was held captive in Lebanon for seven years during the civil war there. In spite of everything he went through, he continued to be a man of deep faith. He subsequently wrote a book of poems on his experience entitled *Den of Lions*. In one of those poems he describes a Eucharist in a Lebanese prison.

> Five men huddled close
> against the night and our oppressors
> around a bit of stale bread
> hoarded from a scanty meal
> and a candle, lit not only as
> a symbol but to read the text by.
> The priest's as poorly clad
> as drawn with strain as any,
> but his voice is calm, his face serene.

The poem concludes:

> The familiar prayers come
> straight out of our hearts.
> Once again, Christ's promise
> is fulfilled; his presence fills us.
> The miracle is real.

His poem is a truly remarkable profession of faith in the Eucharist in an hour of great darkness.

Today's Gospel reading is the conclusion of that long teaching in chapter six of John's Gospel on Jesus as the Bread of Life. Towards the end of that teaching Jesus says, 'My flesh is true food and my blood is true drink. Those who eat my flesh and drink my blood abide in me and I in them.' Jesus is declaring there that he wants to give us the gift of his flesh and blood, the gift of himself. He gave that gift of himself to all humanity on the cross. At every Eucharist he renews this gift of himself to us. Saint Paul declares in his first letter to the church in Corinth, 'As often as you eat this bread and drink this cup, you proclaim the Lord's death until he comes.' Paul recognised very clearly the intimate connection between the Lord's self-gift to us in his death on the cross and his self-gift to us in the Eucharist. It is evident from Terry Anderson's poem that those five men in that Lebanese prison also deeply appreciated the extraordinary gift they were being given in that simple Eucharist. That same self-emptying love of Jesus on the cross was sacramentally present to them in the Eucharist. This is a love through which Jesus gathers people into communion with each other and with himself. It is fitting that one of the terms we have come to use for the Eucharist is 'Holy Communion'. Through the Eucharist, we are brought into a deeply spiritual communion with each other and with the Lord.

The Eucharist is an extraordinary gift from the Lord to us, and yet, today's Gospel shows that some of his own followers were slow to receive this gift. They struggled to accept Jesus' self-gift of his flesh and blood. 'This is intolerable language,' they said. 'How could anyone accept it?' When Jesus spoke of himself as the Bread of Life he had initially met opposition from the Jewish religious authorities. Yet now, the opposition was coming from his own disciples. The Gospel reading goes on to tell us that because of Jesus' teaching on the Eucharist, 'many of his disciples left him and stopped going with him'. I often think that this is one of the more poignant verses in the

Gospels. It can resonate with some of us because there may have been times in our lives when we felt like walking away from the Eucharist. We can do so for a whole variety of reasons. Perhaps, like the disciples in the Gospel reading, we cannot quite bring ourselves to believe in it.

Jesus was helpless before the decision of some of his disciples to leave him. He is profoundly respectful of the mystery of human freedom, even when that freedom expresses itself in ways that are not in keeping with his desire for us. When faced with the Lord's gifts, we can always turn away. At its deepest level, faith is a gift; it is due to the working of God's grace in our lives. Yet, at another level, faith is a choice. The Lord has chosen us first and having chosen us he keeps on investing in us. Yet, he waits for us to respond to his choice of us with our own personal choice of him, a choice we make not just as individuals but within a community. That is why in today's Gospel reading, after many of his disciples had ceased going with him, he turns to the twelve and says, 'What about you? Do you want to go away too?' It is a question that is addressed to all of us; it calls on us to make our own personal choice of the Lord who has chosen us. In response to that question, we can do no better than make our own the answer of Peter, 'Lord, to whom shall we go? You have the message of eternal life.' We give expression to that answer of Peter every time we come to the Eucharist. Our decision to come to the Eucharist every Sunday is a very concrete way of choosing the Lord and all he stands for. In that sense, the Eucharist is both the sacrament of the Lord's giving of himself to us and of our personal and communal giving of ourselves to him.

Twenty-Second Sunday in Ordinary Time

Seeking what is core

Deut 4:1-2, 6-8; Jas 1:17-18, 21-2, 27; Mk 7:1-8, 14-15, 21-3

Etty Hillesum was a young Jewish Dutch woman living in Nazi-occupied Amsterdam during the Second World War. She died in Auschwitz at the age of twenty-nine. She wrote a diary while there and at one point she wrote, 'Every atom of hate we add to this world, makes it more inhospitable … and every act of loving perfects it.' She refused to hate those who had taken everything from her. The essence of her Jewish religious tradition came through in that purity of heart, which she maintained against all the odds.

In today's Gospel reading, Jesus and the Pharisees are in conflict as to what it is that constitutes the true Jewish religion. What is the essence of the Jewish religious tradition? Jesus locates it in what goes on in the human heart and what comes out of the human heart. The Pharisees were more preoccupied with what they called 'the traditions of the elders'. These were concrete observances of various kinds that had been handed down through the generations. Some of them, for example, related to how people should wash their hands before eating, and how vessels that are to be used for eating and drinking should be prepared beforehand. It is evident that Jesus and his disciples did not follow these traditions of the elders very faithfully. The Pharisees accused Jesus and his disciples of not acting in accordance with Jewish religious tradition. They were not being 'religious' in the sense that the Pharisees understood it.

Jesus did not reject Jewish religious tradition. He himself stood very much within it. His concern was to get to the essence of his own religious tradition. The prophets were a very important part of the Jewish tradition and in today's Gospel reading Jesus goes back to one of the prophets, Isaiah, to uncover the essence of the Jewish religious tradition. Jesus quotes God speaking through Isaiah, 'This people honours me only with lip service while their hearts are far from me.' Jesus is saying that the God of Israel wants people's hearts. Their hearts are to be given over to God and to what God wants. This is the purity of heart that Etty Hillesum displayed against all odds. As far as Jesus was concerned, the Pharisees were giving too much importance to what was peripheral in the Jewish tradition and not enough importance to what was central in that tradition. As he says, they were clinging to human traditions while putting aside the commandment of God. They had all the externals of their tradition right but they were missing what was central.

Jesus prompts us to continually seek out the core of our religious tradition. What is it within our own Catholic religious tradition that matters most to God and that speaks to us of God's purpose for our lives? The term 'traditionalist' can sometimes be used in a disparaging way today. Yet, we are all called to be 'traditionalists' in the sense that Jesus would have understood that term. We are to keep in touch with those core elements of our tradition that are a true revelation of God for us today. We find those core elements above all in the scriptures and, especially, in what we as Christians call the New Testament. The scriptures are the primary expression of the Church's tradition. The Second Vatican Council, which took place in Rome in the early 1960s, set itself the task of taking a close look at the various traditions of the Church, and it went back to the scriptures, especially the New Testament, to separate out what was central in all those traditions and what was peripheral, what needed to be retained and what could be changed, just as in the Gospel reading Jesus went back to the prophet Isaiah to do the same. We, the Church, must keep going back to the scriptures to be reminded of what is at the core of our religious tradition and what is less important.

When we do go back to the sources in that way, we discover that there is a strong emphasis on the importance of the heart, the inner core, of the person. If we can somehow get that right, everything else will find its rightful place. In one of his beatitudes Jesus said, 'Blessed are the pure in heart for they shall see God.' He declares blessed those whose hearts are given over to God, those who seek what God wants above all else. Etty Hillesum was certainly among the pure in heart in that sense. In today's second reading, James calls on us to accept and submit to the word that has been planted deep within us. He speaks there of an inner core, a heart, that has been shaped by the word of God. It is from such a heart that will flow what James understands to be authentic religion, namely, supporting those who are most vulnerable among us. Jesus calls for that inner transformation of the heart. This is only possible through the power of the Holy Spirit, the power of God's word. If what is deepest in us is of God, all else will follow.

Twenty-Third Sunday in Ordinary Time   *Lord, open my ears*

Is 35:4-7; Jas 2:1-5; Mk 7:31-7

Some people's hearing deteriorates with the passing of the years. The gradual loss of hearing can become a real burden to them. Something like a loop system, which allows them to hear clearly what is being said at our liturgies with a hearing aid, is much appreciated. There are also people who lose their hearing at a relatively young age. When people suffer from hearing loss it not only has a profound impact on their own quality of life but it also impacts greatly on those around them, especially those who are closest to them. Those among you who live with a loved one who is experiencing severe hearing loss will know that only too well. Those whose hearing is impaired make a particular call on everyone who encounters them. Those of us who have the blessing of full hearing are obliged to make a special effort to communicate with them. We try to express ourselves in a way that makes it easier for the other person to hear us, or we might work at opening up possibilities for them that would not otherwise come their way.

In today's Gospel reading we are given a very good picture of how one man, who had both hearing loss and a speech impediment, was attended to by others in a very striking way. They all lived in a region called the Decapolis, which was a predominantly pagan region on the opposite side of the Sea of Galilee to where Jesus normally lived and worked. When the friends of this man heard that Jesus was in their region, they brought him to Jesus. They did something for him he could not have done for himself. Because of their initiative in bringing their friend into the healing presence of Jesus, he regained both his hearing and his ability to speak. The man's need called forth his friends' attention, and their attentiveness to him helped him to live a fuller life than he could otherwise have lived. Their attentive presence to their friend in his need created a space for the Lord to work in his life.

An inability to hear clearly is only one way that people can make a call on our attentiveness in their need. Indeed, we are all needy in some sense. We are all in need of healing. None of us is complete. Paul, in his letter to the Romans, says that 'the whole creation has been groaning in labour pains until now', and he immediately adds, 'not only the creation, but we ourselves, who have the first fruits of the Spirit, groan inwardly while we wait for adoption, the redemption of our bodies'. Paul is declaring that the whole of creation, including those of us who have received the Holy Spirit in Baptism are groaning inwardly, out of a sense of incompletion. In the words of Isaiah in today's first reading, we are all blind and deaf and lame and dumb, if not in the physical sense, in other deeper senses. We may not all be physically deaf but we are all in need of having our ears opened more fully to the Lord's word and call.

In the scriptures, deafness is often a metaphor for our inability to hear the Lord's call to us and respond to it. Towards the end of the Rite of Baptism the priest says to the child who has been baptised, 'The Lord Jesus made the deaf hear and the dumb speak. May he soon touch your ears to receive his word, and your mouth to proclaim his faith, to the praise and glory of God the Father.' It is an appropriate prayer to pray at the beginning of our Christian lives because we spend the rest of our lives as followers of Jesus learning to receive the Lord's word and to proclaim his faith. Just as Jesus addressed the man in the Gospel reading with the words 'Be opened', so the Lord addresses those words to each of us every day of our faith journey, calling on us to be attentive to his word as it comes to us in the scriptures and from deep within our own heart. The baptismal prayer asks that the Lord touches our ear and our mouth. There is a relationship between how well we listen to the Lord and how well we proclaim him to others. In the Gospel reading, when Jesus opened the man's ears, his power of speech immediately returned. Speaking well, in the Spirit of the Lord, flows from listening well to the Lord's word.

Without the man's friends, who brought him to Jesus, Jesus would not have been able to open his ears and his mouth. There is an image here of the Christian community, the Church. The Lord works through the community of believers. We each have a role to play in helping one another to listen to the Lord's word so that we can proclaim it not just by our lips but by our lives.

Twenty-Fourth Sunday in Ordinary Time

The mystery of the other

Is 50:5–9; Jas 2:14–18; Mk 8:27–35

We are aware from our own experience just how difficult it is to really know someone. Even those who have been sharing each other's lives for many years don't necessarily know each other fully. We can struggle to know ourselves fully, never mind knowing someone else. Even when we know ourselves well, revealing ourselves to others does not always come easy to us. It can be a struggle to reveal ourselves even to those who are closest to us. There is a lot of talk today about transparency; however, no human being will ever be fully transparent to another human being.

When Jesus asked his disciples the question, 'Who do people say I am?' he was checking to see how well people had come to know him. The answers that he received suggested that people had some insight into who he was, although a rather limited one. Jesus was neither Elijah, nor John the Baptist nor one of the prophets, although he had something in common with all of them. Jesus then went on to ask a more probing question of his disciples, 'Who do you say that I am?' Jesus would have expected that his own disciples would have had a fuller insight into his identity. Jesus had chosen them to be with him; they had seen and heard a lot of him. Jesus' expectations were, initially, not disappointed. Peter gave a more satisfactory answer to the question of Jesus' identity than people at large were giving, 'You are the Christ, the Messiah.' Peter was right. Jesus was the long-awaited Jewish Messiah.

However, it soon became clear that Peter did not in fact know Jesus very well. If we struggle to know those closest to us and, even, to know ourselves, it is not surprising that people struggled and continue to struggle to know Jesus. If there is more to each of us than meets the eye or ear, there was certainly more to Jesus than met the eye or ear. The question that Jesus addressed to his disciples, 'Who do you say I am?' is addressed to all of us. We would probably all give somewhat different answers to that question, but one thing is certain, none of the answers would be completely adequate. If coming to know someone close to us is an adventure, a journey with many twists and turns, coming to know the Lord is an even greater adventure and an even longer journey. It is an adventure worth heading into, a journey worth taking on. An important part of our baptismal calling is to come to know the Lord with our head and with our heart. Jesus has revealed himself to us, and continues to reveal himself to us in and through the Holy Spirit. Of course, we will only know the Lord fully when we see him face to face. He will always remain something of a mystery to us on this side of eternity.

Today's Gospel reading shows that, even though Peter showed some insight into Jesus at Caesarea Philippi, Jesus remained a mystery to Peter. Yes, Peter knew that Jesus was the Christ, the Messiah, but he had no idea about the kind of messiah that Jesus would become. Immediately after Peter's moment of insight into Jesus, Jesus went on to reveal a little more about himself. He spoke of himself as the Son of Man who was destined to suffer grievously, to be rejected by the religious leaders of the time, and to be put to death. This was not the kind of messiah Peter had in mind, and so he took Jesus aside and began to rebuke him. Peter had his own image of Jesus and what Jesus was saying did not fit that image. Peter's reaction to Jesus is not unlike how we react to each other. We can have a certain image of people, and we expect them to fit that image. When they show themselves to be more mysterious, more complex, than our image of them, we can be slow to accept them. Peter struggled to accept a messiah who had to travel the way of the cross. Perhaps he understood that following such a messiah would mean that he himself would have to travel that same way of the cross. However, Jesus cannot be fully understood apart from the cross. His death reveals who he is more fully even than his life. His death reveals Jesus to be someone who was totally faithful to God and to all God's people; it is above all his death that reveals the quality of Jesus' love for God and for all of us. It is not surprising then that the cross has become the dominant symbol of Christianity.

Because Jesus had to travel the way of the cross, he calls on us, his followers, to take up our cross after him. Taking up our cross is not passively accepting every misfortune that comes our way. The language of 'taking up our cross' suggests freely choosing the cross. Following Jesus, remaining faithful to him and to his values, will always mean freely choosing the more loving path for his sake. The more loving path will often be the more difficult path, the way of the cross, but it will also be the path of life, both for us and for others.

Twenty-Fifth Sunday in Ordinary Time

God-inspired ambition

Wis 2:12, 17–20; Jas 3:16–4:3; Mk 9:30–37

We can all struggle at times to listen to someone. It can be especially difficult to listen to people when they are sharing something with us that we find difficult to hear. They may be sharing some painful experience that is troubling and disturbing. We struggle to listen to their story because it arouses painful emotions in us. Someone might be trying to tell us something about ourselves that we find difficult to hear. We struggle to face the truth that is being put to us; we tune it out. We can also find ourselves reading something that forces us to question some of our convictions and beliefs. Again, we can easily find ourselves tuning out, putting the book down. In all sorts of ways, we can be tempted to keep at bay whatever we find unsettling or disturbing.

That very human tendency is reflected in the behaviour of the disciples in today's Gospel reading. Jesus had something very important to say about what was about to happen to him. He was telling his disciples that he would be delivered into the hands of others and that they would put him to death. This was something that they found very hard to hear. There was a truth here that they were not able to take on board. According to the Gospel reading, 'They did not understand what he said and they were afraid to ask him.' This was the second time in Mark's Gospel that Jesus told his disciples what was likely to happen to him. They were no more open to hearing it the second time than they were the first. They did not understand what he said and they were reluctant to question him because they were afraid. They were afraid that they might not be able to live with the answers he would give them. In some ways that is a very human reaction. We often find ourselves not willing to ask questions because we suspect that we would struggle to live with the answers to our questions.

Yet, in our heart of hearts, we often recognise that there are certain realities we need to face, even if they are painful. There are certain illusions we may have to let go of, even if we have come to cherish them. In the second part of today's Gospel reading Jesus worked to disillusion his disciples. He needed to prise them away from the illusions of greatest that they harboured. They seemed to have thought that being part of Jesus' circle would bring them privilege and status. No sooner had Jesus spoken of himself as someone who would end up as one of the least than the disciples began to argue among themselves as to which of them was the greatest. They wanted power and, it seems, that they wanted power for its own sake. This is the kind of self-centred ambition that James talks about in the second reading when he says, 'You have an ambition that you cannot satisfy, so you fight to get your way by force.' In place of that very worldly ambition, Jesus places before his disciples a very different kind of ambition, an ambition that has the quality of what James in that reading refers to as 'the wisdom that comes down from above'. This is God's ambition for their lives and for all our lives. It is the ambition to serve. As Jesus says in the Gospel reading, 'Those who want to be first must make themselves last of all and servant of all.' This ambition to serve, again in the words of James in that second reading, is something that 'makes for peace and is kindly and considerate; it is full of compassion and shows itself by doing good'.

Jesus implies that this is to be our primary ambition as his followers. All our other ambitions must be subservient to that God-inspired ambition. Jesus elaborates on his teaching to his disciples by performing a very significant action. He takes a little child and sets the child in front of his disciples, puts his arms around the child and declares that whoever welcomes one such child, welcomes him and not only him, but God the Father who sent him. Jesus was saying by that action that the ambition to serve must give priority to the most vulnerable members of society, symbolised by the child who is completely dependent on adults for his or her well-being. Our ambition is to serve those who, for one reason or another, are not in a position to serve themselves. Jesus assures his disciples and us that in serving the most vulnerable we are in fact serving him. In the presence of the disciples who seemed consumed with an ambition for power for its own sake, Jesus identifies himself with the powerless, those who are most dependent on our care. Over against the ambition of the disciples to serve themselves, Jesus puts the ambition to serve him as he comes to us in and through the weakest members of society. In our Gospel reading Jesus is putting before us what his family of disciples, the Church, is really about.

Twenty-Sixth Sunday in Ordinary Time

The Spirit blows where it wills

Num 11:25-9; Jas 5:1-6; Mk 9:38-43, 45, 47-8

Rivalry is inevitable in human relationships. Sometimes it is to be encouraged because it is appropriate and normal, such as in competitive sport. The rivalry between teams and individuals in various sports is the lifeblood of the professional game. Healthy rivalry between companies, whether it is in the food industry, the travel industry or any other domain of commercial life, can work to the benefit of the consumer. Rivalry between educational establishments can promote a richer and more diverse learning environment for students. There are other forms of rivalry that are recognised to be dangerous. Rivalry between nations to have the most powerful nuclear weapons is rightly judged to be a threat to world peace. Gang rivalry in cities can result in mayhem and even death. Rivalry between closely connected communities for domination can lead to open warfare.

The first reading and the Gospel reading for this Sunday highlight a form of rivalry that is not necessarily as destructive as the last set of examples, but is not judged to be healthy either. A young man runs to Moses, clearly disturbed that two men are showing evidence of the Spirit of God in their lives, even though they do not belong to the group of the seventy who are officially recognised to have received the Spirit from God. The young man saw these two men as potential rivals of the seventy. Moses' reply to the breathless concern of this young man was, 'If only the Lord gave the Spirit to all the people.' In the Gospel reading, John, one of the twelve, was very concerned that someone who had not been officially sent by Jesus was engaged in a healing ministry in Jesus' name. Jesus' reply to John's concern about this potential rival was, 'Anyone who is not against us is for us.'

In both stories people of faith held that certain individuals were rivals and were to be discouraged, whereas, in the eyes of God, they were helpers to be encouraged. Both episodes bring home to us that God's perspective on things can be much broader than our perspective. The people we might judge to be some kind of threat to the ways of God, in reality, may be serving the ways of God. The comment of John is revealing: 'Because he was not one of us, we tried to stop him.' 'One of us' is equivalent to 'one of the twelve'. John took the role of the twelve whom Jesus had appointed very seriously, as did Jesus himself; however, John took the role of the twelve too seriously. The difference between taking ourselves seriously and taking ourselves too seriously can be very significant.

We take ourselves seriously as a church. We believe ourselves to be the sacrament of Christ in the world, the place where Christ and his Spirit can be experienced in a privileged way. Yet, the Church itself teaches that God's Spirit is not confined to God's church. There is a real sense in which, as Jesus says to Nicodemus, 'the Spirit blows where it wills'. The Church is the fullest sign of God's kingdom; however, when the Church identifies itself with God's kingdom, it risks becoming triumphalist and elitist. Signs of God's kingdom are to be found outside the Church, in the lives of all men and women of good will. The readings invite us to rejoice in goodness, self-giving service, the pursuit of truth and justice, wherever such values are to be found, because, when those values become real in people's lives, there God is present, there the Spirit is at work, and God's purpose for our world is becoming more of a reality. As Paul writes to the Philippians, 'Whatever is true, whatever is honourable, whatever is just, whatever is pure, whatever is pleasing, whatever is commendable … think about these things.'

Most parishes have a variety of groups working to serve the Lord in a variety of ways. That variety is itself very important. The purpose of God is so rich and the love of God so wide and deep, that only a great variety of groups within a faith community can give adequate expression to God's loving purpose. John had to learn that the group of the twelve alone, important as they were, could not serve God's will adequately. It goes without saying that the clergy cannot do this either. The Spirit will generate a whole variety of groups within a faith community to further the coming of God's kingdom. We are called to welcome this variety, rather than eyeing other groups as rivals to ours. If any one group is clearly serving the Lord, we all rejoice.

There is nothing elitist about the kingdom of God. Jesus promises that 'people will come from east and west, from north and south, and will eat in the kingdom of God'. This diverse group will surely include many who may not have been recognised in this life as doing God's work. It may even include some who may have been hindered in the doing of this work because they were judged not to belong to the right group. In the light of today's readings, we pray for God's breadth of vision that allows us to recognise the Spirit of God at work, wherever that may be.

Twenty-Seventh Sunday in Ordinary Time
Jesus' vision of marriage

Gn 2:18–24; Jas 2:9–11; Mk 10:2–16

The relationship between science and religion has been very much to the fore in recent years. That relationship has often been expressed as one of conflict; for example, between scientists who hold to an evolutionary view of the emergence, of the world and its life forms and creationists who hold that the world was created just as the Book of Genesis says it was. However, many scientists and religious believers have come to recognise that there is no real conflict between science and religion. The Bible is not a scientific book and does not make scientific claims. It makes different kinds of claims, in language that is often highly symbolic, claims about God and about God's relationship with us and our relationship with God and each other.

The story of the creation of man and woman by God in the second chapter of the Book of Genesis, a section of which we have in today's first reading, is not a scientific account of the creation of the human couple. Rather, it is a symbolic description of the relationship between man and woman, and between them and God. According to Genesis, God created man from the earth and God created woman from the side of man. This account of the creation of woman has often been misinterpreted to suggest the subordination of woman to man. The woman was created second, not first; she was taken from the man's side to be his helpmate. However, that is to misread the text. 'Helpmate' is not an accurate translation of the Hebrew word. Something like 'indispensable partner' would be better. The text suggests that the woman is to stand alongside the man as his equal. She corresponds to him exactly, as the man affirms, 'bone of my bones, flesh of my flesh'. Though the man names the animals, suggesting a certain authority over them, he does not name the woman. The primary relationship between the man and the woman is adult human to adult human. The text proclaims that from the beginning God intended men and women to relate to one another with mutuality and partnership. According to our first reading, that relationship of mutuality and partnership between a man and a woman finds its fullest expression in marriage, a 'man leaves his father and mother and joins himself to his wife, and they become one body'.

In today's Gospel reading, Jesus turns to this text from the Book of Genesis when he is put on the spot by some Pharisees regarding the question of divorce. As the Pharisees would have known, the Jewish law permitted a form of divorce. According to the Book of Deuteronomy, a man who becomes displeased with his wife because he finds in her something objectionable could write her a bill of divorce, hand it to her and dismiss her from his house. There was no provision in Jewish law for a woman to divorce her husband. It was a law which left women vulnerable. In reply to the Pharisees, Jesus declares that what the law allows is not actually what God wills. God's purpose for marriage, according to Jesus, is to be found in those opening chapters of the Book of Genesis. The Pharisees ask Jesus about divorce, but in his reply Jesus places the focus on marriage. His vision of marriage is of a profound union between a man and a woman, a communion of faithful love. It is no coincidence that immediately after the passage in which Jesus speaks of marriage, Mark in his Gospel gives us a story about children, about parents bringing children to Jesus for him to bless them. Marriage between a man and a woman is a tried and tested way in which children can grow up to be loved, as well as being given stability and security. No other setting has been proven better for the nourishing and flourishing of children. If society cares about children, it will channel financial and professional resources into supporting marriage, understood as a communion of faithful love between a man and a woman, the fullest expression in human form of the communion of love between the Lord and ourselves.

We know from our own experience that not all marriages reflect the ideal that Jesus places before us in today's Gospel reading. We all know marriages that have not lasted. The Gospels are clear that although Jesus presented a certain vision for human relationships, including within marriage, he did not condemn those who fell short of that vision. All of us, married or single, are called to love one another as the Lord has loved us, and we all fail in our response to that call. It is in those moments of weakness and failure that the second part of today's Gospel reading has most to say to us: 'Anyone who does not welcome the kingdom of God like a little child will not enter it.' We stand before the Lord with a childlike heart, in our weakness and vulnerability, open and receptive to the great gift of the Lord's love that is given to us unconditionally. It is that gift which empowers us to keep reaching towards the goal, the ideal, that Jesus puts before us all.

Twenty-Eighth Sunday in Ordinary Time

Standing before the Lord's call

Wis 7:7-11; Heb 4:12-15; Mk 10:17-30

As parents know, children are great for asking questions. They have a way of asking big questions in a very unselfconscious way. 'Where does my cat go when he dies?' 'Who made God?' As adults, we continue to ask probing questions, questions of meaning. In today's Gospel reading, a man of great wealth puts one such question to Jesus, 'What must I do to inherit eternal life?' The importance of this question to him, and his anxiety to have it answered, is suggested by his running up to Jesus and falling at his feet. This was a question that mattered to him. I suspect it matters to all of us. This man of great wealth was clearly a good man. He lived by the values of the Ten Commandments. He took his religious duties seriously. Yet, he sensed that there was something missing in his relationship with God. There was some restlessness in him that led him to put his urgent question to Jesus.

Many of us might feel that we have a lot in common with this man. We may not have his wealth, but, like him, we are probably doing our best to live well. We are trying to live by the values of the Gospel. Again, like him, there are probably times when we feel that there must be something more to the living of our faith. We can experience that restlessness which makes us ask questions of ourselves, of others, of God. If we do feel such restlessness from time to time, it is a sign that we have remained open to the Lord's call to us. On one occasion Jesus said, 'Seek and you will find, knock and the door will be opened to you.' People who are open to God's call will always be seekers; they will always be looking beyond where they are at any particular time. People of faith never cease to ask probing questions; they learn to live with such questions because they are always on the way; they are never fully settled.

The Gospel reading tells us that Jesus looked upon the rich man with love and confirmed to him that there was something lacking in his life, just as he had suspected, saying, 'There is one thing you lack.' Even though this man was lacking in his relationship with God, Jesus looked on him with love. The Lord looks on us all with love, even though we may not yet be all he is calling us to be. Jesus went on to issue a challenging call to the man, asking him to sell all his possessions, to give the resultant money to the poor, and then to follow him wherever he led. There is no record in the Gospels of anyone else being asked to do precisely what Jesus asked of this man. The command to sell everything and give it to the poor and physically follow Jesus was this man's personal calling from the Lord. The man discovered, to his sadness, that he could not respond to this call. Having asked his question, he couldn't live with the answer he was given. Having run to Jesus with a spring in his step, he walked away sad.

We can all feel some sympathy for this man's inability to respond to the Lord's call. Even if we have not been given the precise call from the Lord that this wealthy man was given, the Lord looks upon each one of us with love, and he keeps calling us into a deeper relationship with himself, a fuller following of him. He is always prompting us to go and do something, and to do it today. We may be aware of the times when we said 'no' to this call. We may have experienced the sadness that often comes over us when we turn away from some worthwhile path because we sense that it would involve having to let go of something we are clinging to.

Often my hesitation before the Lord's call to take an extra step can come from a sense that I am not able for this; however, when the Lord calls us, he does not leave us to our own abilities. In calling us, he also enables us. As Jesus says in today's Gospel reading, 'For people it is impossible, but not for God: because everything is possible for God.' When the Lord calls us, he invites us to rely on the strength that he gives us. The wealthy man in the Gospel reading had perhaps come to rely too much on himself, on his own possessions. His initial question could be heard as, 'What must *I* do to inherit eternal life?' Jesus suggests that the emphasis is not to be placed so much on 'what I must do' but, rather, on what the Lord can do in me and through me. This is the spirit of today's responsorial psalm, where the psalmist prays, 'Lord, give success to the work of our hands.' Responding to the Lord's call does involve work on our part, but the success of that work has more to do with the Lord than with us. He enables us to do what we cannot do on our own. From the moment of our Baptism, his Spirit is at work in our lives. Our baptismal calling is to allow that Spirit to empower and shape us as we follow the Lord's very personal call to each of us.

Twenty-Ninth Sunday in Ordinary Time
In what does greatness consist?

Is 53:10-11; Heb 4:14-16; Mk 10:35-45

The iconic boxer Muhammad Ali, or Cassius Clay as he was known before, had a habit of saying 'I am the greatest'. No one took exception to this statement because it was generally acknowledged that among heavy weight boxers he was indeed the greatest. He also said, 'I am the greatest', with a smile on his face, as if, deep down, he wasn't taking himself too seriously. However, there have been others who have laid claim to being the greatest with devastating consequences for humanity. The absolute ruler who considers himself the greatest and will allow no challenge to his supreme authority can be a terrifying phenomenon. The question 'Who is the greatest?' is never far from us. An even more significant question is 'In what does greatness consist?'

The Gospel reading suggests that the question 'Who is the greatest?' was alive and well among Jesus' first disciples. The brothers, James and John, who were among the first disciples called by Jesus, took their opportunity to stake their claim to being the greatest among the disciples. They asked Jesus for the best seats in his glorious kingdom, immediately to the left and right of his throne. The other ten members of the twelve are described as being 'indignant' at James and John. They were annoyed that James and John had gotten their request in ahead of all the others. The potential gain for James and John would mean a loss for everyone else. Competition among Jesus' first disciples for the best places in Jesus' glorious kingdom appears to have been very keen.

Jesus does not grant the request of James and John and then immediately addresses the indignation of the other ten. Whereas the disciples were concerned with the question, 'Who is the greatest?' the more important question for Jesus was 'In what does greatness consist?' In the previous chapter of Mark, Jesus had already given clear teaching on what greatness in God's kingdom looks like. The disciples had been arguing with one another as to who was the greatest. In response to their concern with the question, 'Who is the greatest?' Jesus went on to give a teaching on what 'greatness' really consists in, from God's perspective. He declared on that occasion, 'Whoever wants to be first must be last of all and servant of all.' As an example of the kind of service he is talking about, Jesus took a little child, placed his arms around the child and declared, 'Whoever welcomes one such child in my name welcomes me.' Service consists above all in welcoming and caring for the most vulnerable. This teaching of Jesus appears to have fallen on deaf ears, as is evidenced by today's Gospel reading. Once again, Jesus makes clear how greatness is understood in God's kingdom, 'Anyone who wants to become great among you must by your servant, and anyone who wants to be first among you must be slave to all.' Being a servant to others will often entail the way of the cross, which is why Jesus asked James and John, 'Can you drink the cup that I must drink, or be baptised with the Baptism with which I must be baptised?' Jesus' faithfulness to the service of all required that he drink the cup of suffering; it entailed his being plunged into a sea of suffering.

It is only when we have answered the question, 'In what does greatness consist?' that the question, 'Who is the greatest?' can be answered. Jesus defines greatness by his self-emptying love of others. As he declared at the end of the Gospel reading, he came not to be served but to serve and to give his life as a ransom for others. Saint Paul captures this truth about Jesus when he says of him that he 'emptied himself, taking the form of a servant'. The truly great people among us are those who serve others in a selfless way, without looking for anything in return. We can all identify such people in our own minds. If we encountered such people during our lives, we will have been greatly blessed by them. There will have been occasions in our own lives when we will have risen to this form of greatness. These are the times when we gave ourselves to others at some cost to ourselves, without their being any obvious benefit to ourselves. The Gospel reading suggests that such selfless service of others did not come easy to Jesus' first disciples and, it does not always come easy to us either.

The second reading declares that the Lord understands our weakness because he was tempted in every way that we are. Indeed, in the Garden of Gethsemane, Jesus was strongly tempted to turn off the path of self-emptying service, because he saw clearly where it was leading him. Yet, he resisted the temptation and renewed his commitment to the path he had taken since his Baptism. It is because the Lord knows our struggle to be great in the way he has defined greatness that we can be confident in approaching the throne of grace, in the words of that second reading. There we can be sure of finding mercy when we fail and grace to help us keep travelling the Lord's path of self-emptying service of others.

Thirtieth Sunday in Ordinary Time   *The seeing of faith*

Jer 31:7-9; Heb 5:1-6; Mk 10:46-52

A blind man was invited to attend a friend's wedding. The couple were being married in a village church that was well known for its picturesque qualities and its beautiful grounds. The guests commented on all of this at the reception afterwards and again when the photos came back. They were struck by how well the church, the grounds and the setting all looked. When the blind man heard all this talk he thought to himself, 'But didn't they hear the bell?' For him, the bell that pealed to welcome the bride and celebrate their marriage had been magnificent. The air was filled with its vibrating jubilation. He was amazed at the atmosphere of joy and solemnity that the bell created for the occasion. Everyone else seemed to have missed that part of the ceremony. Although he could not see, perhaps because he could not see, his hearing was very alert. He heard the beauty that others missed. The sounds that passed others by touched him very deeply.

Today's Gospel reading is the story of a blind beggar. Although he was blind, his hearing was very sensitive. The Gospel reading says that he heard that Jesus of Nazareth was passing by. Although he could not see, the beggar was aware of the presence of Jesus because of his heightened sense of hearing. He cried out, 'Jesus, Son of David, have pity on me.' Even when people around Jesus, including perhaps some of Jesus' disciples, told him to keep quiet, he shouted all the louder, 'Son of David, have pity on me.' Even though he could not see Jesus, he was determined to make contact with him through this urgent prayer from his heart. His prayer was an act of faith. He recognised Jesus as 'Son of David', which was one of the titles for the Messiah, and trusted that Jesus could heal his blindness. By making contact through his hearing and his speaking, he revealed that he had an inner sight. Even though he was blind, he saw Jesus with the eyes of faith. Even when he was rebuked by the crowd for confessing his faith out loud, he refused to be silenced. He had the courage to keep professing his faith, in spite of the hostility and scorn it brought upon him.

This man's faith literally brought Jesus to a standstill. The Gospel reading says simply, 'Jesus stopped.' Jesus' response to the heartfelt prayers of this man was in complete contrast to that of the people around him. Rather than telling him to keep quiet, Jesus told those around him to call him over. Jesus is portrayed as the champion of those not considered worthy enough to come near to God. Again, we witness the extraordinary responsiveness of this man to Jesus' presence, to the call of Jesus. When he heard that Jesus was calling him, he threw off his cloak. His cloak, no doubt, served many purposes. It sheltered him from the weather, it was his bed, it was in a sense his home. Yet, he abandoned it, and having done so, he jumped up and went unerringly to Jesus in his blindness. Nothing was going to hold him back from connecting with Jesus, not even his precious cloak. He speaks to all of us of our own need to free ourselves of the binds that stifle our faith and keep us from approaching the Lord. The question that Jesus asked him when they came face to face was not the kind of dismissive question that comes from annoyance at being interrupted, 'What do you want?' Rather, it was a very personal question 'What do you want me to do for you?'

It is a question that we can all hear as addressed to each of us personally, and how we answer that question can reveal a great deal about who we are and what we value. In the passage in Mark's Gospel that immediately preceded this one, Jesus asked that same question of two of his own disciples, James and John, 'What do you want me to do for you?' Their answer revealed a self-centred ambition, 'Grant us to sit, one at your right hand and one at your left, in your glory.' The blind man's answer to Jesus' question revealed a very different heart. Aware of his blindness, aware of his disability, he asked simply, 'Master, let me see again.' In answering his prayer, Jesus addressed him as a man of faith, saying 'Your faith has saved you.' He was already seeing Jesus with the eyes of faith before he received back his physical sight. Once he received back his physical sight, we are told that he followed Jesus along the road. He immediately used his newly restored sight to walk after Jesus as a disciple up to the city of Jerusalem, where Jesus would be crucified. His faith had shaped his hearing and his speaking, and now it shaped the path he would take. We could do worse than take this man as a model for our own journey of faith. Like him we are blind beggars who need to keep on crying out to the Lord who passes by, so that we can see him more clearly and follow him more nearly.

Thirty-First Sunday in Ordinary Time

Where is the core to be found?

Deut 6:2–6; Heb 7:23–8; Mk 12:28–34

One of the tasks we all have in life is trying to distinguish what is more important from what is less important. We wonder what needs to be at the centre of our lives and what can move out towards the edge. This can be true of our faith life too. We ask ourselves what is it that is central to what we believe. Some beliefs are core and others less so. From its earliest days, the Church found it necessary to list its core beliefs. This led to the formation of the creeds, which we recite every Sunday. In the creeds the Church was laying out its core beliefs. In the time of Jesus, there was a similar concern among Jews to get to the core of their faith. There were six hundred and thirteen commandments in the Jewish law. People wanted to know what was really important among these commandments and what was less important. This concern is behind the question put to Jesus in today's Gospel reading, 'Which is the greatest commandment of the law?'

The questioner was looking for one commandment out of the hundreds that were in the law. However, Jesus did not give him one commandment, but two, what he called the greatest or first commandment and another commandment that resembles it. In focusing on the core of the Jewish law, Jesus found it necessary to highlight two commandments. It seems that Jesus did something very original here. He took two commandments that were in different books of the Jewish scriptures, the first commandment that you love the Lord your God with all your heart, soul, mind and strength, which is in the Book of Deuteronomy, and the second commandment, 'you must love your neighbour as yourself', which is in the Book of Leviticus. Jesus brought these commandments together in a way that had never been done before. What is common to both commandments is that little word, 'love'. It is as if Jesus is saying that when you boil down what it is that God wills for our lives, it is love. Love is the centre of the Jewish law. It is also, of course, the centre of Jesus' message.

If what unites these two commandments that were originally quite separate is the word 'love', what distinguishes them is the object of our love. In this respect, Jesus speaks of a first and a second commandment. These two commandments to love are the most important of all the commandments in the Jewish law and one is more important than the other. The first and most important of the two is to love God with all our heart, all our soul, all our mind and all our strength. I think it is fair to say that we probably find it easier to get our head around the second commandment, to love our neighbour as ourselves. We may not find it easy to do, but we understand what it means. We might ask who our neighbour is. Jesus answered that question in the parable of the good samaritan. We are to treat everyone as if they were a neighbour, including the stranger who crosses our path, whoever they are. That parable suggests that rather than trying to figure out who is and isn't my neighbour, the important thing is to be a neighbour to all who cross our path in life, without discrimination. That is the kind of love Jesus understands the second commandment to be referring to, a love he expressed in his own life. He related to people out of love, whoever they were.

This is a very demanding kind of love, and this brings us to the first commandment, which has to do with our relationship with God. Jesus seems to be saying that it is our relationship with God that will empower us to love others in this generous way. That is why loving God with all our heart, soul, mind and strength is the first and greatest of the commandments. Yet, we struggle a little to grasp what it is to love the invisible God. Indeed, in the secular world in which we live, that first commandment tends to be disconnected from the second and often abandoned altogether. In that first commandment, we are being asked to give God first place in our lives. God alone is to be loved with all our being. This involves acknowledging our dependence on God, recognising how much we receive from God and then offering all that back to God in love. Saint Ignatius of Loyola had a strong sense of how much he had received from God and a great desire to give it all back to God. This comes through in one of his well-known prayers, 'Take, Lord, and receive all my liberty, my memory, my understanding, all my will – all that I have and possess. You, Lord, have given all to me. I now give it back to you.' That prayer captures something of this all-embracing love of God that Jesus calls for in the first commandment. This love of God is the inspiration and foundation for our love of others.

Thirty-Second Sunday in Ordinary Time   *When a little is all*

1 Kgs 17:10–16; Heb 9:24–8; Mk 12:38–44

Most of us probably have negative memories of school or college examinations. Coming up to exams is always a time of pressure. We often come away from exams with a feeling that we may not have done ourselves justice. Examinations are very much part and parcel of college and school life. Yet, many feel that they are a limited means of assessing knowledge and understanding. That is one of the reasons why various forms of continuous assessment have become more popular in school and college life. End of year examinations are probably better at assessing ability than at assessing effort. Very able people who may not do much work can do very well in examinations, whereas those who work hard but are less able for the exam format can do poorly.

There is not always a close relationship between ability and effort, between what people have and what they give. Some who have a lot can be very sparing with what they give. Others who have a little can be very generous in their giving. The first reading and the Gospel reading focus on two widows who had very little but gave a great deal. In the first reading, the widow only had a handful of meal in a jar and a little oil in a jug, which was barely enough for herself and her son. Yet, she shared the little she had with the prophet Elijah when he asked for help. The widow in the Gospel reading had even less to her name. All she possessed in the world was two small coins, the equivalent of a penny, which at the time was about one thirtieth of a day's wage. Yet, little as she had, she put the whole lot into the temple treasury. Her extraordinary generosity revealed the depth of her surrender to God and, indeed, her complete trust in God to provide for her. She had very little to give and, yet, she gave everything. Those who had an abundance of this world's goods put much more into the temple treasury than she did. Yet, relatively speaking, they put much less into the temple treasure, because after they made their generous contribution, they continued to have a great deal left, whereas after she made her tiny contribution, she had nothing left.

Jesus is suggesting that generosity is not so much measured by what we give as by what we have left after we give. The widow gave her all; she had nothing more to give. Even though the economic value of what she gave was tiny, the value of what she gave in the Lord's eyes was enormous. When Jesus looked at her and drew the attention of his disciples to her, he may have recognised something of himself in her. At this point in Mark's Gospel, Jesus is in the temple in Jerusalem. Very soon he will undergo his passion and death. In the course of that painful final journey, he himself will give everything he has. Everything will be taken from him. By the time he cries out, 'My God, my God, why have you forsaken me?' he will have nothing more to give. Like the widow before the temple treasury, he will have given everything he possessed. It is with this poor woman that Jesus identifies, and not with the religious leaders that Jesus spoke about earlier in the Gospel reading, those who like to walk around in long robes and take the front seats in the synagogues. In contrast to the external signs of honour sought out by the religious leaders of the day, this poor widow possessed true honour in God's eyes. Jesus also says of these religious leaders that they make a show of lengthy prayers as a cover for swallowing the property of widows. It is somewhat ironic that this widow gives so generously to an institution that exploits her.

This passage prompts me to ask, 'Where would Jesus recognise something of himself today? To whom would Jesus draw our attention today?' The Gospel reading suggests that he would recognise himself most of all in those who, like the widow in the Gospel reading, mostly go unnoticed, but whose total trust in God enables them to give without counting the cost, without looking to see what they have left, without expecting anything in return. They don't just give of their possessions, but they give of themselves. It is said of Jesus in the second reading that he sacrificed himself, he offered himself. God is more interested in the gift of ourselves than in the gift of our possessions. Jesus saw something of himself in the widow. Through Baptism we become members of Christ's body, temples of his Spirit; we are to live our lives in such a way that Jesus recognises something of himself in us, especially in our generosity and goodness of spirit. We pray today that through the grace of Baptism we will keep growing into the kind of person Jesus recognises as an image of himself.

Thirty-Third Sunday in Ordinary Time   *The Lord at the gates*

Dn 12:1-13; Heb 10:11-14, 18; Mk 13:24-32

A few years ago the front gates of the church were taken away to be worked on by a professional company. They are very old gates and they were no longer hanging properly. When you tried to open or close them, they scraped along the ground. Standing near the gates of the church is a good place to meet people as they enter or leave the church. This is why collectors stand at the gates of the church, and, I suppose, why coming up to an election politicians stand outside the gates of the church. Gates have traditionally been places where people gather. This was especially true in times past when towns and cities were surrounded by a wall, perhaps not so much in Ireland but certainly in the land of Jesus. In a walled city or town, the gate was the only point where people can enter or leave. It was the place to meet people. If you wanted to address the largest number of people possible, the gate of the city or town was the place to go. In the Jewish scriptures, there is a figure called Wisdom, a female figure. She has a message that she wants as many people as possible to hear. The Book of Proverbs states, 'Beside the gates in front of the town, at the entrance to the portals, she cries out.' She obviously wanted to reach as many people as possible, and so she went to the gates of the town.

That image of the gates is in today's Gospel reading. Jesus speaks there of the coming of the Son of Man, clearly a reverence to himself, and he declares, 'Know that he is near, at the very gates.' Jesus uses that image of his presence at 'the very gates' to suggest his nearness to us. He will be present where people gather, not in some remote place, but at the very place where the largest number of people come and go. His presence at the gates is a reassuring presence. He had just used the reassuring image of the fig tree that had been bare for the winter and whose twigs suddenly begin to grow supple and whose leaves begin to emerge into the light. When people see this happening, they know that winter is passing and summer is approaching. The image of Jesus at the gates is meant to be a similarly reassuring image. Some kind of reassurance was needed because Jesus had just been painting a disturbing picture of great cosmic changes and, in the passage just prior to our Gospel reading, he had spoken of the destruction of Jerusalem and its temple and the persecution of his followers. It was a rather grim and dark picture of what lay ahead. Jesus did not shy away from facing and naming the harsh realities of life, the suffering which lay ahead for himself and his followers and, indeed, for the whole of creation. We can only begin to deal with the darker side of life when we name it for what it is and face into it as best we can. The Gospels suggest that Jesus was better at this than his disciples, who were inclined to change the subject when Jesus spoke to them about such darker matters.

Yet, while acknowledging and naming the darker side of reality, Jesus also pointed to a light in that darkness. He assures his disciples that when the world as they know it appears to be collapsing, he will be coming with great power and glory to gather those who remain faithful to him. He will be the reassuring presence at the very gates of their city, their town, their household, their lives. The message of today's Gospel reading is essentially one of hope. Hope is not wishful thinking; it is not pretending that things are better than they are. Hope is the conviction that God's light shines in the awful darkness and that the darkness will not ultimately overcome it. Jesus is acknowledging in the Gospel reading that everything as we know it is passing away. All of created reality is destined to pass away. Nothing of this world will endure. As Jesus says, 'Heaven and earth will pass away.' The term 'heaven and earth' was a way of referring to everything created that exists. Jesus immediately goes on to say, 'My words will not pass away.' His words will not pass away because he himself will not pass away. In our darkest moments when our world appears to be collapsing, when what we cherish most has been taken from us, he will be at the gates of our lives as a light in our darkness, as a companion on our way. In the Book of Revelation, the risen Lord uses an image that is very similar to the one in today's Gospel reading, 'I am standing at the door, knocking; if you hear my voice and open the door, I will come in to you and eat with you, and you with me.' The Lord moves from the gate or the door to the table where he invites us to enter into communion with him and draw life from him, and then go forth as his hope-filled messengers in our often disturbed and fragile world.

Our Lord Jesus Christ, Universal King *The King of Truth*

Dn 7:13-14; Apoc 1:5-8; Mk 18:33-7

This feast brings to end the Church's liturgical year. Next Sunday, the first Sunday of Advent, is the beginning of a new liturgical year. The feast of Christ the King has always had a particular meaning for me. My home parish was dedicated to Christ the King. On the outside of the church, above the side door, stands a huge stone statue of Christ the King. I believe it was made in Italy and was transported from Italy to be erected on the outside of the church shortly after it was built in about 1930. The statue made an impression on me as a child. It was on a grand scale; it was clearly made to impress.

Yet, as a king, Jesus was not impressive in the way earthly kings and rulers tend to be impressive. It is noteworthy that, in the Gospels, it is only when Jesus enters the journey of his passion that the title 'king' begins to be applied to him. It is only then that we consistently hear the title, King of the Jews, with reference to Jesus. The inscription over the cross read, 'Jesus of Nazareth, King of the Jews'. It was intended as a joke, as a mockery. In today's Gospel reading we have a small section of the exchange between Jesus and Pilate as it is given to us in the Gospel of John. If the title 'king' was to be applied to either of those two men, Pilate would be the much more likely candidate. He was representing the most powerful empire on earth; he was Caesar's man in Judea. Jesus was a handcuffed prisoner, who was facing death by crucifixion. In terms of how the world understood kingship, Jesus was as far from being a king as one could imagine. Yet, in that dialogue with Pilate, Jesus does speak of his kingdom, and declares to Pilate, 'Yes, I am a king.'

However, it is obvious that he is not a king in any sense in which that word would have been understood then. He declares that his kingdom is not of this world. That does not mean that it is purely spiritual with no connection to the material world. It means that it is constituted on a totally different basis to the kingdoms of this world. It is not a kingdom that needs defending by force of arms; it does not impose itself on others by military means. Jesus explains to an uncomprehending Pilate that he exercises his kingship by witnessing to the truth. Earlier in John's Gospel, Jesus had said, 'I am the truth.' He is the truth, he witnesses to the truth, in the sense that he reveals the truth about God; he shows us who God is, what God is like. He reveals the truth about humanity; he shows us what it is to be human, how to live a fully human life, because he himself was the most fully human person who ever lived. He reveals the truth about our world, about creation, the cosmos, the universe. He gives us the light, the divine light, which allows all of reality to be seen for what it really is. Jesus exercises his kingship by witnessing to the truth.

That means that we submit to his kingship by receiving the truth that he communicates to us. We show ourselves to be his subjects by seeking the truth, by never giving up on our search for truth, the truth about God, about ourselves, about our universe. Sometimes that search takes people away from Jesus and from the Church in and through which, for all its failings, we meet Jesus. Yet, if we remain faithful to our search for truth we will eventually come to the Lord. I came across a quotation from Simone Weil recently that I found very thought-provoking. She was a French philosopher and a social activist who, as her life progressed, became more religious and moved in the direction of mysticism. She wrote, 'One can never wrestle enough with God if one does so out of pure regard for the truth. Christ likes us to prefer truth to him because, before being Christ, he is truth. If one turns aside from Christ to go towards the truth, one will not go far before falling into his arms.'

The truth that Jesus brings is not a merely theoretical doctrine that satisfies the mind. It is a truth that can transform our lives. Earlier in John's Gospel Jesus had said, 'If you continue in my word ... you will know the truth and the truth will make you free.' The Gospel contains a liberating truth which, if we surrender to it, will help to make our lives more human. If Jesus is the King of Truth, our calling as his followers is to be people of truth. If he is the faithful witness, as the second reading declares, the faithful witness to the truth, then our mission in life as his followers is to be faithful witnesses to the truth he proclaimed and lived. We are to be truthful in what we say, what we write, how we live. In John's Gospel, when Jesus saw Nathanael coming towards him, he said, 'here is a man incapable of deceit', or in another translation 'a man in whom there is no guile'. It would be wonderful if the Lord could say that of each one of us.